BUILDER-TESTED | CODE APPROVED

WINDOWS & DOORS

FROM THE EDITORS OF **Fine Homebuilding**

The Taunton Press

The Taunton Press
Inspiration for hands-on living®

The Taunton Press Inc., 63 South Main St., PO Box 5506, Newtown, CT 06470-5506

e-mail: tp@taunton.com

Cover Design: Alexander Isley, Inc.

Layout: Cathy Cassidy

Front Cover Photographer: Brian Pontolilo, courtesy *Fine Homebuilding,*
© The Taunton Press, Inc.

Back Cover Photographer: © James Kidd

Taunton's For Pros By Pros® and Fine Homebuilding® are trademarks of
The Taunton Press Inc., registered in the U.S. Patent and Trademark Office.

Library of Congress Cataloging-Publication-Data

Windows & doors / from the editors of Fine Homebuilding.
       p. cm. -- (Taunton's for pros by pros)
    Includes index.
    ISBN-13: 978-1-56158-808-4
    ISBN-10: 1-56158-808-3
    1. Windows--Maintenance and repair--Amateurs' manuals. 2. Doors--Maintenance and repair--Amateurs' manuals. I. Title: Windows and doors. II. Fine Homebuilding. III. For pros, by pros
    TH2270.W634 2006
    690'.1822--dc22

                    2005029672

Printed in the United States of America
10 9 8 7 6 5 4 3 2 1

The following manufacturers/names appearing in *Windows & Doors* are trademarks: American Architectural Manufacturers Association™, Andersen®, B-I-N®, Caradco®, Dacron®, Fortifiber™, Häfele®, Jeld-Wen®, Kreg®, Loewen®, Macklanburg-Duncan®, Makita®, Marvin®, Masonite®, Moistop®, National Fenestration Rating Council™, *New Yankee Workshop*®, Owens Corning®, PBS™, Pella®, Q-LON®, Schlegel®, Stanley®, Titebond II®, Weyerhaeuser®, Zinsser®

Special thanks to the authors, editors, art directors, copyeditors, and other staff members of *Fine Homebuilding* who contributed to the development of the articles in this book.

CONTENTS

PART 2 : WINDOWS

INTRODUCTION

In a new house, the windows and exterior doors typically cost more than anything else. More than the lumber. More than the flooring. Even more than the kitchen cabinets and appliances. Unless those windows and doors are installed meticulously, they're the most likely places for water to leak and rot to gain a toehold. And even if they are installed meticulously, the windows and doors will be the biggest energy wasters in the house, driving up utility bills. Makes you wonder why we bother.

But windows and doors are the difference between a home and a prison. They provide light, air, views, and access to the outdoors. In his landmark book on architecture *A Pattern Language*, Christopher Alexander even says that for a room to be comfortable it must have windows on at least two sides. You need walls and a roof to create shelter, but you need windows and doors to make a great place to live.

In this book we've collected 21 articles from past issues of *Fine Homebuilding* magazine, all of which deal with windows and doors—choosing them, building them, installing them, fixing them. Written by builders, these articles represent hard-won knowledge and years of experience. Because they're often called on to remodel homes, builders see first-hand what has and hasn't worked. You'd be hard pressed to find better advice than what's collected here.

—Kevin Ireton, editor,
Fine Homebuilding

Installing Prehung Doors

■ JIM BRITTON

Of all the tasks a trim carpenter faces, few offer the opportunity to transform the look of a house quickly from ragged edges to finished surfaces like installing prehung doors. It's the trim carpenter's version of instant gratification because once in the groove, a good trim carpenter can install a door, its jamb, and all the casings in about 15 minutes. That's money in the bank for a pro, and a satisfying slice of sweat equity for the owner/builder.

But doors that squeak, bind, stay open or swing open by themselves are constant reminders of the fallibility of the trim carpenter. In this chapter I describe the methods I've settled on after 20 years in the trades for efficiently installing a typical prehung door and avoiding common glitches that bedevil a door installation. Like most home-building jobs, installing a door begins with checking work done before you got there.

Check the Rough Opening First

In a perfect world of accurate levels, conscientious framing crews, and straight lumber, all rough openings are square, plumb, and correctly sized. Because these three condi-

tions rarely coincide, it falls to the trim carpenter to compensate for less-than-perfect rough openings.

Although there are exceptions, the rough opening should be 2 in. wider and 2½ in. taller than the door. Thus the correct rough opening for a 2-ft. 6-in. door would be 32 in. by 82½ in. The extra space allows room for the door jambs and a little wiggle room to accommodate rough openings that are out of plumb. In my experience, rough openings are the same for both interior and exterior doors that are made by door manufacturers. Doors made by window manufacturers, on the other hand, sometimes require a different rough opening. If in doubt, check with the manufacturer before the framers start work.

Before installing a door, I inspect the rough opening to familiarize myself with its condition. First I check the dimensions to see if they are workable. Then I use a 6-ft. level to check that the two trimmers (the studs that frame the rough opening) are plumb in both directions (see photos 1 and 2). Sometimes the trimmers will actually be plumb in both directions, in which case the door jambs will be flush to the wall, and the casings will be easy to install.

But in some situations, the wall will be out of plumb in section, with the trimmers plumb in elevation. In this case, the door jambs will have to protrude slightly beyond the plane of the wall at the top and bottom on opposite sides.

Another common condition is the parallelogram-shaped rough opening. The wall may be plumb in section, but the elevation view of the rough opening is out of plumb. The net door width is usually ½ in. narrower than the rough opening. Therefore, I can install a plumb door in a rough opening that is up to ½ in. out of plumb. The jambs will fit snugly to the diagonally opposite corners of the rough opening. If the rough opening is more than ½ in. out of plumb, I use a sledgehammer to pound the trimmers into line. I can usually move a trimmer up to

1 and 2. Read the rough opening. Before installing the door and its jamb, the author checks the trimmers on both sides of the rough opening with a 6-ft. level to see if the trimmers are plumb. If the jamb needs to project beyond the plane of the wall in order for the door to hang plumb, he notes the direction of the adjustment on the trimmer. To avoid mistakes, he marks on the floor the direction the door will swing.

3. Check the trimmers for twist. If the trimmer isn't square to the header, the door jamb will also be askew. Use a square to gauge the accuracy of the door frame.

½ in. without adversely affecting the drywall. This operation requires cutting back the sole plate once the trimmer has been adjusted.

The scissor condition, in which the trimmers are out of plumb in opposite directions in section, requires a more involved solution. Let's say one trimmer is ½ in. out top to bottom in one direction, and the other trimmer is out ½ in. in the other direction. This situation amounts to 1 in. of scissor. This condition is remedied by holding the jamb out ¼ in. at the top and in ¼ in. at the bottom on opposite sides of the wall. Do the opposite for the other trimmer.

The other condition I look for is twist (see photo 3 on p. 5). If the trimmers aren't square to the header, the jamb will likewise be twisted. This condition results in hinge binding or a poor visual relationship between the door and its jamb after the installation. I take the twist out when I affix shims to the trimmer.

Next, Put Up the Hinge Shims

To begin an installation, I measure the height of the top and bottom hinges of the door from the bottom of the hinge jamb. My 6-ft. level makes a convenient stick to note the middle of the hinge positions (see photo 4). These locations mark where I fasten my shims to the framing before the door goes in.

I shim the bottom location first with an appropriate combination of shims to bring the level plumb and to compensate for any twist in the trimmer. Then I move to the top hinge position, holding the shims in place with my level as I affix the shims to the trimmer (see photo 5). Prenailed shimming makes handling the door easy and ensures that the door will automatically be plumb in the elevation view. I use a 15-ga. or 16-ga. pneumatic nailer loaded with 1¾-in. to 2-in. nails for installing prehung doors. If

you don't have one of these wonderful time-saving tools, use 8d finish nails instead.

Now it's time to squeeze the door and jamb into the opening. Remove any nails or straps used as bracing, and place the hinge jamb atop the thick end of a shim resting on the floor next to the trimmer (see photo 6). Raising the jamb has three benefits: It eliminates squeaks by separating floor and jamb, it eliminates the problem of an out-of-level floor preventing the strike jamb from not coming down far enough to engage the lockset latch, and it eliminates (or minimizes) the need to remove some of the door's bottom to accommodate finish flooring.

Once the jamb is in the rough opening, I swing open the door. If it's a troublesome installation, I'll block the door with a couple of shims. But typically I leave the open door unsupported. If the wall is plumb at the rough opening, I bring the edge of the hinge jamb flush with the drywall and nail it to the trimmer through the shims. If the wall isn't plumb, I compensate for the error by moving the jamb out equal amounts at the bottom and then the opposite direction at the top. I make pencil marks on the shims to note the correct alignment for the edge of the jamb (see photo 7).

I affix the jamb in the correct position relative to the wall with a couple of nails through the top and bottom shims. Then, while the door is still open, I drive a couple of nails through the jamb right next to the hinges (see photo 8). The hinge jamb and door now should be hanging plumb because they are held fast against the shims. If there is a middle hinge, shim it at this time, taking care not to make any changes to the already perfect alignment.

Nails are enough to keep the jamb of a hollow-core door from pulling away from the trimmer. But if I'm hanging a solid-core door, I run a 2½-in. screw through the jamb and into the trimmer next to each hinge. Because this step leaves a hole that no painter will be pleased to discover, I put the screws

4

6

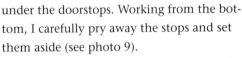

5

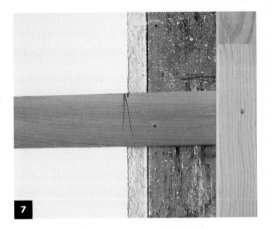

7

8

9

CHECK THE ROUGH OPENING FIRST

4. Note the hinge positions. Using a 6-ft. level as a story pole, the author marks the centers of the top and bottom hinges.

5. Affix the shims. Shims behind the top and bottom hinges make backing for the jamb. A single shim at the top compensates for twist.

6. Don't forget the shim on the floor. Elevate the hinge jamb by placing it atop the butt end of a shim shingle as the door is lifted into position.

7. Mark the jamb alignment on the shims. If you need to adjust the edge of the jamb in or out of the plane of the wall to get the door to hang plumb, make a note of the correct position of the jamb's edge on the top and bottom shims.

8. Nail the jamb. Secure the jamb to the trimmer with a couple of nails right next to the hinges. The nails must pass through the shims.

9. Remove the stops. Pry the doorstops from the bottom up. Then locate the screws that secure the jamb to the trimmer under the stop.

under the doorstops. Working from the bottom, I carefully pry away the stops and set them aside (see photo 9).

I sometimes run a 2½-in. screw through a hinge and into the trimmer. But I don't do this to keep the door from sagging: A properly hung door doesn't sag. Instead, I use the longer screw to straighten a warped jamb or to compensate for a hinge mortise that might be shallow. The longer screw will give me about 1/16 in. of adjustment.

10. Equalize the strike-jamb reveal. Use shims placed next to the door latch to adjust the strike jamb in or out until the gap is consistent from top to bottom.

11. Reinforce the strike plate. After pulling the doorstop, run a screw through the strike jamb next to the door latch.

10

11

Secure the Head Jamb and Strike Jamb

Now that the hinge jamb is firmly secured to its trimmer, I close the door. Next, I set the head jamb parallel to the top of the door by raising or lowering the strike jamb. At this stage of the game, a single, unshimmed nail through the strike jamb into its trimmer or through the head jamb into the header can help hold the parts in alignment while I assemble the correct combination of shims. A jamb held by a single nail still can be pried in or out as needed. A shim under the strike jamb also can be helpful.

When I've got the head jamb parallel with the top of the door, I check the reveal along the edge of the door and the strike jamb. I put a couple of shims between the jamb and the trimmer 6 in. down from the head jamb and adjust the shims until the gap, or reveal, between the door and the jamb is the same at the top corner. Then I shim the bottom of the jamb, 6 in. from the floor, and the center of the jamb opposite the strike plate (see photo 10). Some door jambs are straighter than others. If I've got one with some dips and wows in it, I add shims as necessary to keep the reveal consistent. I add extra support to the jamb where the strike engages it. To do so, I pry away the doorstop and drive a 2½-in. screw into the trimmer (see photo 11).

Replace the Doorstop

The door is now where I want it and fully supported. With the door closed flush with the head jamb, I position the head stop on the hinge-jamb side with the help of a dime (see photo 12). This ¹⁄₁₆-in. gap between the door and the stop helps keep the door from binding on the stop and allows for paint buildup. I continue this space down the hinge jamb with the hinge stop, attaching the stop with my 16-ga. nails, 16 in. on center.

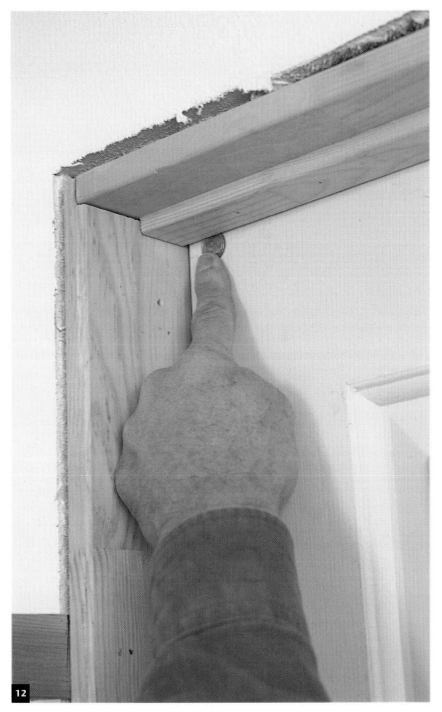

12

REPLACE THE DOORSTOP
12. Don't forget the stop gap.
Use a dime between the closed door and the doorstop to gauge a consistent gap between the door and the stop. The gap allows for paint buildup.

I install the strike stop so that it just touches the entire height of the door with the door's face and the jamb flush over the full height. This system works well for a strike that has an adjusting tang. However, if the strike will be the T-mortise type, it will have to be installed first and the stop set to it.

Apply the Casings Last

I start casing a door at the top with the head casing set back ³⁄₁₆ in. from the edge of the jamb (see photo 13 on p. 10). The casing has 45-degree miters on each end, and the short side of the casing is ³⁄₈ in. longer than

APPLY THE CASINGS LAST

13. Casing starts at the top. The author begins trimming a door by installing the head casing first. He affixes the casing with pairs of nails on 16-in. centers. One nail goes into the jamb, and another into the header.

14. This gap won't make the cut. When the door jamb and the wall are in slightly different planes, the casings don't lie completely flat. The tapered gap at the inside corner is the result.

15. Undercut the side casing. With the side casing face-side up and slightly tilted, the author removes material from the miter cut with a bench-mounted disc sander.

the jamb opening. That gives me the 3/16-in. reveal along both of the side jambs.

The tricky part of casing a door is dealing with the differential between the plane of the wall and the plane of the jambs when you've made allowances for an out-of-plumb rough opening. For example, this door had a head casing whose edge was recessed a bit from the plane of the wall. When I test-fit the side casing, I came up with a gap at the inside corner (see photo 14). To fix it, I undercut the miter with a disc sander (see photo 15). This cut isn't a back bevel, however. In this case I removed material

from the casing's face. Once I'd shaved the miter, I had an acceptable joint for paint-grade trim work (see photo 16). To keep the adjoining casings in the same plane at the outside corner, I put a thin shim under them (see photos 17 and 18).

I attach the side casings with pairs of nails, one into the jamb and one into the trimmer a couple of inches away. This nailing pattern helps ensure that the casing will lie flat. I nail the casings next to the hinges and the door strike because these spots are well-backed by shims. Nailing the casing at these points also reinforces the jamb.

16. Now it fits better. By undercutting the side casing with the disc sander, the author achieves an acceptable miter. A dose of caulk will touch up the remaining crevices.

17. Shim problem casings at the corners. If the casings are out of plane, slip a shim under the corner so that both pieces bear on it. Then trim the shim flush with the casing with a utility knife.

18. Nail 'em. Once the shim has been trimmed, secure the casing corners to the wall with nails driven into the header, trimmer, and door jamb. Fill any gaps between the wall and the casing with caulk.

As you can imagine, drywall edges can be a pain in the neck when the door jamb is below the plane of the wall. The hollow milled into the back of the casing is there to compensate for this situation. If the hollow isn't enough to accommodate the drywall, I use my hammer to "tenderize" protruding drywall edges.

If the floor is to be covered with carpet, I hold the side casings ⅜ in. above the floor. That gap gives the carpet guy some room to tuck the edges of the rug. It's a good idea to put a shim between the jamb and the trimmer at the bottom of the jamb if the room is to be carpeted. The shim keeps the jamb from being deflected by the carpet layer's bump hammer as he tightens the carpet against the tack strips.

If the floor is going to be finished with ¾-in. hardwood strips, I set the side casings on ¾-in. blocks. When the floor is installed, the blocks come out, and the flooring slips into the gap.

Jim Britton is a trim carpenter and a contractor living in Fairfield, California.

A New Door Fits an Old Jamb

■ GARY M. KATZ

I used to hate hanging doors. It's way too easy to make a mistake, like hinging the door backward or upside down, or planing the bevel in the wrong direction. And I always had a tough time making a ⅛-in.-to-zero cut across the top of a door, especially if the door cost more than all my tools combined and especially if someone was watching me work.

But years of hanging doors and learning from professional door hangers have tempered my views. In fact, the techniques that I outline here can make door hanging foolproof and fun, even if you're hanging your first door. Using just a few simple tools and following the steps in order, you'll no longer need to be afraid of doors—or of people watching you work on them.

Gary M. Katz is a carpenter living in Reseda, California, and the author of The Doorhanger's Handbook *(The Taunton Press, 1998).*

1. Shims Position the Door in the Opening

Scribing the door to the opening is an important first step. Start by setting the door on a couple of shims, then hooking it against the top of the jamb (see the photo on the facing page). A homemade door hook holds the door against the jamb (see the drawing at right).

Adjusting the shims raises or lowers the door to the right position. If the head of the jamb is out of level, raise or lower one side of the door until the top rail is parallel to the jamb head. A small prybar moves the door until it's centered in the opening (see the photo below), but I leave at least $3\frac{7}{8}$ in. on the lock stile after planing; otherwise, some dead bolts might not fit. If the head is out of level and the jamb can't be fixed easily, cheat the door a little out of plumb to make the head look better.

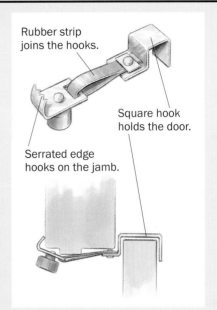

Rubber strip joins the hooks.

Square hook holds the door.

Serrated edge hooks on the jamb.

2. Mark the Door Edges

Use a simple set of dividers to scribe the edges of the door. Because I'm on the stop side (see the photo at right), I spread the dividers to $3/16$ in. (for a $1\frac{3}{4}$-in. door) to account for the hinge gap as well as bevels on both edges. If I'm fitting an interior door, I scribe the bottom of the door for the floor it swings over. For standard carpet, I spread the scribes to $1\frac{3}{8}$ in. An exterior door is scribed for the threshold and door shoe (see the photo and the drawing below).

Before taking down the door, make a large *X* out of tape on the hinge-side top of the door to orient it once you've carried it to the door bench. Also measure for each hinge location. I used to transfer hinge locations from the jamb to the door by eye, but because the trim often keeps the door $1/2$ in. away from the jamb, it's hard to keep the marks perfectly level. Careful measurements eliminate guesswork.

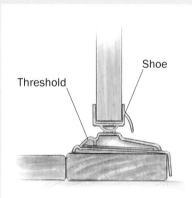

Threshold

Shoe

3. Trim the Top and Bottom First

A door bench is helpful when working on a door, but sawhorses also can be used. After placing the door flat with the X facing up, score the cut-line across the stiles with a razor knife to prevent tearout. Cut about $\frac{1}{16}$ in. wide of the line, using a sharp blade in your circular saw (see the photo above). Then plane right to the line. I start with the plane upside down, stopping within a foot of the opposite end so that I don't blow out the back edge of the stiles (see the photo at right). After planing to the line, turn the plane right side up and finish the other end with no blowout. While the door is lying flat on the bench, seal the top and bottom.

4. Bevel and Mortise the Hinge Edge

Set the door on edge with the X facing the bench to plane the hinge stile. Plane to the scribe line with the plane set to about a 3-degree bevel (see the photo below and the drawing on the facing page). The bevel prevents hinge binding. I also ease the edges with the plane at a 45-degree angle.

Lay out the hinges with a tape measure and look for the X to make sure you lay out the mortises from the top (see the top right photo on the facing page). The hinge barrels should point away from the X. For speed and accuracy, I use router templates for all hinge and hardware mortises (see the bottom left photo on the facing page). To keep the hinge screws from splitting the stile, drill pilot holes with a centering bit before attaching the hinges (see the bottom right photo on the facing page).

3-degree
bevel

5. One Flip Is All You Need

Because I keep the scribe lines and the X facing the door bench at all times, I flip the door vertically, not horizontally, to work on the opposite edge, the lock stile (see the left photo above). Bevel the lock stile with the plane at the same 3-degree bevel (see the top right photo above). Then measure for the lock bore, again remembering to look for the X so that you measure from the top instead of the bottom. Because

I install lots of doors, I've invested in a lock-boring jig, although a paddle bit and a hole saw also can work well. Drill and mortise for the lockset (see the bottom right photo above), then carry the door back to the opening. About 95 percent of the time, the door fits the first time I swing it.

6. Final Tweak for a Perfect Fit

To hang the door, tip it until the top screw hole in the top hinge lines up with the screw hole in the jamb, and drive that screw. Align the door by pushing with your foot, and drive the rest of the screws in the hinges (see the top photo at left).

When the door is swinging from the jamb, check the fit. Doors often need tweaking because hinges aren't all the same. To move the door toward the strike jamb, place a nail set between the hinge leaves and against the hinge barrel (see the bottom left photo at left), then close the door gently. The nail set spreads the hinge slightly.

To move the door toward the hinge jamb, first pop up the hinge pin until it's just engaging the top barrel. Then tighten an adjustable open-end wrench around each of the barrels on the hinge leaf attached to the door (see the bottom right photo at left). Use the wrench to bend the hinge toward the strike side. This will close the gap on the hinge side.

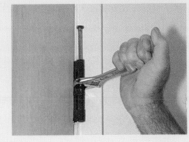

Installing a Split-Jamb Door

■ BRUCE ABERNATHY

Door manufacturers keep making it easy on us. As an improvement to building door jambs on site, they gave us prehung doors: doors that are hinged and installed in the jamb at a factory. No more building jambs or mortising hinges. All that's left to do is set the door in an opening and install trim pieces. How could they make it any easier? By installing the trim at the factory, too.

Split-jamb doors, featuring tongue-and-groove jambs with casing already applied, answered the prayers of overextended trim carpenters and do-it-yourself homeowners somewhat daunted by tight miter joints.

The jamb with the groove, called the split jamb, contains the door and door stops and is installed first. The tongued half, called the main jamb, is installed second. The tongue-and-groove design ensures a tight fit, even when wall thickness changes due to bulges in plaster or drywall.

My method for installation involves preplumbing the rough opening with custom shims. I can go from rough opening to finished casing in less than a half hour.

Shims and Spacers Remove the Guesswork

Because precased doors leave no room for shims to extend beyond the wall, standard shims don't work easily for split-jamb doors. Instead, I cut 4-in. by 4-in. square shims from ⅛-in., ¼-in., and ½-in. stock; and plumb the rough opening on the hinge side before setting the jamb in place (see photo 1 on p. 24).

If I'm installing a door before the finished floor is in place, I use a variety of spacers to raise the jamb off the floor. For carpet, I use a ⅜-in. spacer; for tile, I use a ½-in. spacer; and for hardwood or an engineered floor, I ask the floor installer for samples of flooring, and I use the samples as spacers.

Doorways often define transitions between floorings of different thickness. Split-jamb doors make this transition easy.

Like a jamb sandwich. Cased on each side, the jamb's tongue-and-groove design sandwiches the wall and can mask variations in wall thickness.

MAIN JAMB
The tongue side is installed last.

SPLIT JAMB
The grooved side has the door, stops, and hinges.

The Split-Jamb Prehung Door

Advantages:

- Installs quickly.

- The jamb can conform to changes in wall thickness.

- Comes with casing (or trim) already installed.

- The split jamb can be adjusted to remove slight gaps between the door and the stop due to uneven rough openings.

- This style is easily adaptable to floor-thickness transitions.

Disadvantages:

- Home centers have a limited selection of molding styles.
  Local door makers and lumberyards will install any casing style you want.

- Not as strong as solid jambs.

A Story Pole Makes It Quicker

I verify the rough-opening size and determine the direction of door swing. This step establishes which side the hinge jamb is on.

The rough opening should be 2 in. taller and 2 in. wider than the door size: 82 in. for a 6-ft. 8-in. door and 98 in. for an 8-ft. door. This space allows room for the jamb, shims, and clearance for the floor covering.

I cut a straight 2x4 to create a simple story pole for marking the door's hinge positions. The 2x4 should be shorter than the rough opening and taller than the top hinge. Number and location of hinges vary by manufacturer, so I make a new story pole for each job. I attach a 4-ft. level to the story pole with shrink wrap. I like shrink wrap because it's fast and leaves no sticky residue as tape does.

Setting a spacer on the floor on the hinge side of the rough opening, I stand the story pole against the trimmer stud and plumb it by fastening premade shims at the hinge

locations. I'm usually installing an entire houseful of doors, so I plumb all the rough openings before installing any doors.

Install the Split Jamb First

I separate the jambs and place each jamb on its proper side of the rough opening. For shipping, the door usually is secured to the jamb with one or more nails. Because the door is easier to handle with a nail in place, I remove all the nails but one, which I loosen.

Setting the hinge side on the floor spacer, I test-fit the split jamb in the rough opening. If it fits, I slip the latch side out, pull the last nail, slip the latch side back into the rough opening, and tack the casing at the hinges. I prop open the door at about 90 degrees to expose the hinges. With the casing snugly against the wall and the jamb pushed tight against the shims, I drive a #9 by 2½-in. screw through the top hinge to lock the jamb to the framing. I do the same to the

Standard Prehung Door

Advantages:

- Far quicker to install and more accurate than a blank door and jamb, which must be assembled, hinged, and fitted on site.
- Usually, wide walls can be accommodated with extension jambs to the nonhinged side.
- One-piece jambs are strong.

Disadvantages:

- If the wall is not of uniform thickness, a gap will appear between the casing and the jamb.
- The casing needs to be installed.

bottom hinge and middle hinge. The common #8 screws are too small and #10 screws are too big, so I search out #9 screws.

With the door secured to the wall on the hinge side, the head and latch jambs hang loose. Remaining on the door side, I close the door and slip ⅛-in. spacers between the jamb and the door to produce a uniform gap across the top of the door and along the latch side. Then, I nail the casing tight to the wall (see photo 2 on p. 25).

It's important not to use a floor spacer under the latch jamb for three reasons: The latch holes are measured from the top of the door, the jamb legs may not be the same length, and the floor may not be level.

Slip the Tongue into the Groove

Now that the door and split jamb are installed, I close the door. From the latch side, I fill the gap between the jamb and the trimmer stud. Using precut shims, I gently fill this space at the top, bottom, and latch

plate. Because the jamb is exactly where it is supposed to be, the shims should snug the jamb to the trimmer stud but not move the jamb. It is better to err on the loose side than to pack the gap too tight.

With the shims at the top, bottom, and latch, I slip the main jamb into the split jamb (see photo 4 on p. 24). I hold the casing of the main jamb firmly against the drywall and nail it off.

Once this step is done, I nail through the jamb where the tongue and groove mate (see photo 6 on p. 25). Don't overcompress the door jamb at this point; an air-powered finish nailer does the trick nicely. I nail through the shims on the latch side and at each hinge. If there are only two hinges on the door, I add a nail where the middle hinge would be.

Bruce Abernathy *(www.bruceabernathy.com) is a trim carpenter in Niceville, Florida.*

Split Jamb (Groove Side)

1. Prepare the rough opening. With precut shims, plumb the hinge side of the rough opening. If the jack stud is plumb already, use three shims at the hinge locations to center the door in the opening. To make sure the shims line up properly with the hinges, set the level/story pole on a spacer of the same thickness as the flooring.

2. Screw hinges into the framing. After inserting the split jamb into the now-plumb opening and tacking the casing to the wall, remove the center screw from each hinge and replace it with a longer one to penetrate the framing. Although not common, #9 screws fit better than #8 or #10 (see the bottom right photo on the facing page).

3. Tight-fitting spacers make a uniform gap. Placed at the top, latch, and bottom of the split jamb, ⅛-in. spacers maintain a uniform gap between door and jamb while the casing is nailed.

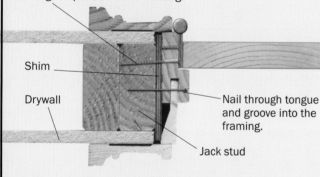

Replace the middle screw in each hinge with one long enough to penetrate the framing.

Shim

Drywall

Nail through tongue and groove into the framing.

Jack stud

Main Jamb (Tongue Side)

4. Slip the tongue into the groove. Gently fill the gap on the latch side with spacers before slipping the tongue into the groove. Set the hinge-side tongue on the floor spacer, and slide the rest into place. Omit a flooring spacer on the latch side; the reveal around the door has been set.

5. Nail the casing. Hold the casing tight against the wall and nail it with a 2½-in. finish nail into the jack stud every 2 ft. or so.

6. Nail the split jambs. A final nailing sequence through the door stops and into the jack studs joins the tongue and groove together. Nail through the jambs at the top, bottom, and center hinge locations. If the door has only two hinges, add a third nail in the center.

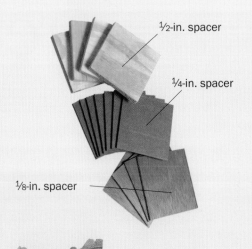

DIFFERENT SHIMS FOR SPLIT JAMBS
Because split-jamb doors have preapplied molding, long, wedge-shaped shims won't work; instead, the author cuts 4-in. squares of different thicknesses to plumb the opening, to raise the jamb for flooring, and to make a consistent gap around the door.

½-in. spacer

¼-in. spacer

⅛-in. spacer

SCREW THE HINGES TO THE FRAMING
For a sturdy installation, remove the middle screw from each hinge and replace it with one long enough to penetrate the framing. The hard-to-find #9 screws fit the countersink perfectly.

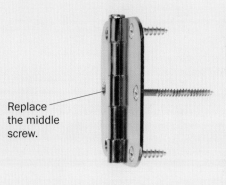

Replace the middle screw.

Hanging French Doors

■ GARY STRIEGLER

The old adage "Children should be seen and not heard" must have been coined by a French-door salesman. Most people I know like French doors. They're an elegant way to cordon off rooms without visually separating them. In fact, they act more like windows between rooms than doors.

Hanging French doors, however, can be frustrating. Getting two doors, either of which may be slightly warped, to meet up perfectly when installed in the almost certainly imperfect framing of a house requires several levels of adjustment. Correcting the rough opening or fixing an out-of-plumb or cross-legged opening might call for the use of a sledgehammer, which doesn't take much technical skill. Making adjustments for an out-of-level floor or a bowed door, on the other hand, takes a little more finesse.

Gary Striegler is the principal of Striegler and Associates, a custom-home contractor in Fayetteville, Arkansas.

Two doors are harder than one. The trick is setting one jamb leg plumb and just tacking the other before hanging the doors and finally adjusting the second side perfectly.

Assessing the Rough Opening

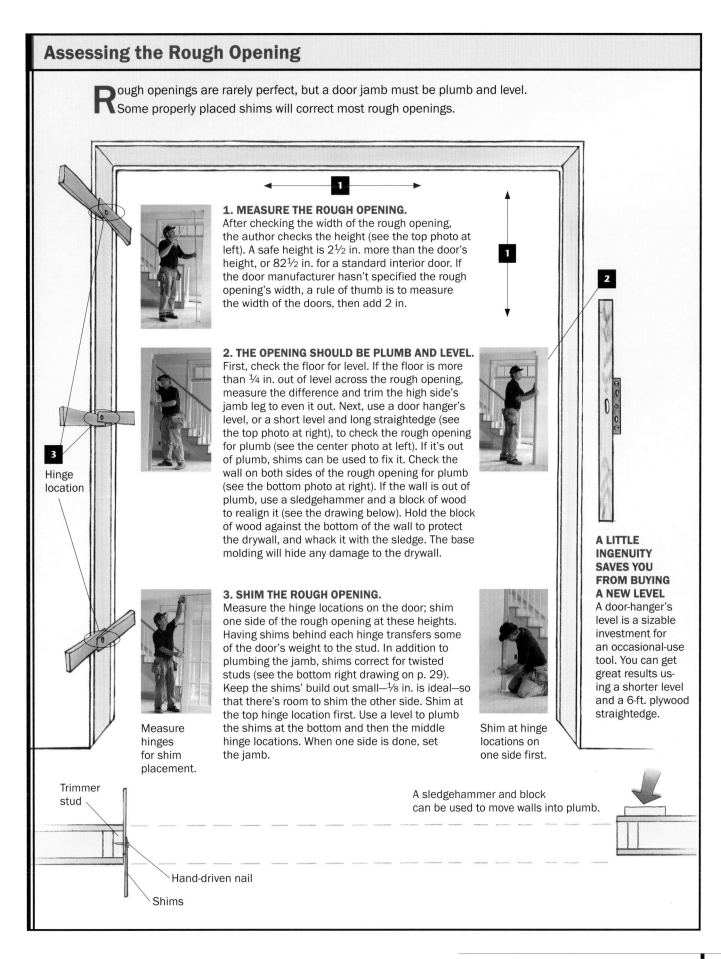

Rough openings are rarely perfect, but a door jamb must be plumb and level. Some properly placed shims will correct most rough openings.

1

1

2

1. MEASURE THE ROUGH OPENING.
After checking the width of the rough opening, the author checks the height (see the top photo at left). A safe height is 2½ in. more than the door's height, or 82½ in. for a standard interior door. If the door manufacturer hasn't specified the rough opening's width, a rule of thumb is to measure the width of the doors, then add 2 in.

2. THE OPENING SHOULD BE PLUMB AND LEVEL.
First, check the floor for level. If the floor is more than ¼ in. out of level across the rough opening, measure the difference and trim the high side's jamb leg to even it out. Next, use a door hanger's level, or a short level and long straightedge (see the top photo at right), to check the rough opening for plumb (see the center photo at left). If it's out of plumb, shims can be used to fix it. Check the wall on both sides of the rough opening for plumb (see the bottom photo at right). If the wall is out of plumb, use a sledgehammer and a block of wood to realign it (see the drawing below). Hold the block of wood against the bottom of the wall to protect the drywall, and whack it with the sledge. The base molding will hide any damage to the drywall.

3. SHIM THE ROUGH OPENING.
Measure the hinge locations on the door; shim one side of the rough opening at these heights. Having shims behind each hinge transfers some of the door's weight to the stud. In addition to plumbing the jamb, shims correct for twisted studs (see the bottom right drawing on p. 29). Keep the shims' build out small—⅛ in. is ideal—so that there's room to shim the other side. Shim at the top hinge location first. Use a level to plumb the shims at the bottom and then the middle hinge locations. When one side is done, set the jamb.

3

Hinge location

Measure hinges for shim placement.

Shim at hinge locations on one side first.

A LITTLE INGENUITY SAVES YOU FROM BUYING A NEW LEVEL
A door-hanger's level is a sizable investment for an occasional-use tool. You can get great results using a shorter level and a 6-ft. plywood straightedge.

Trimmer stud

A sledgehammer and block can be used to move walls into plumb.

Hand-driven nail

Shims

With one side of the rough opening plumbed, set the jamb. Additional shimming will be necessary to fine-tune the jamb for a perfect fit.

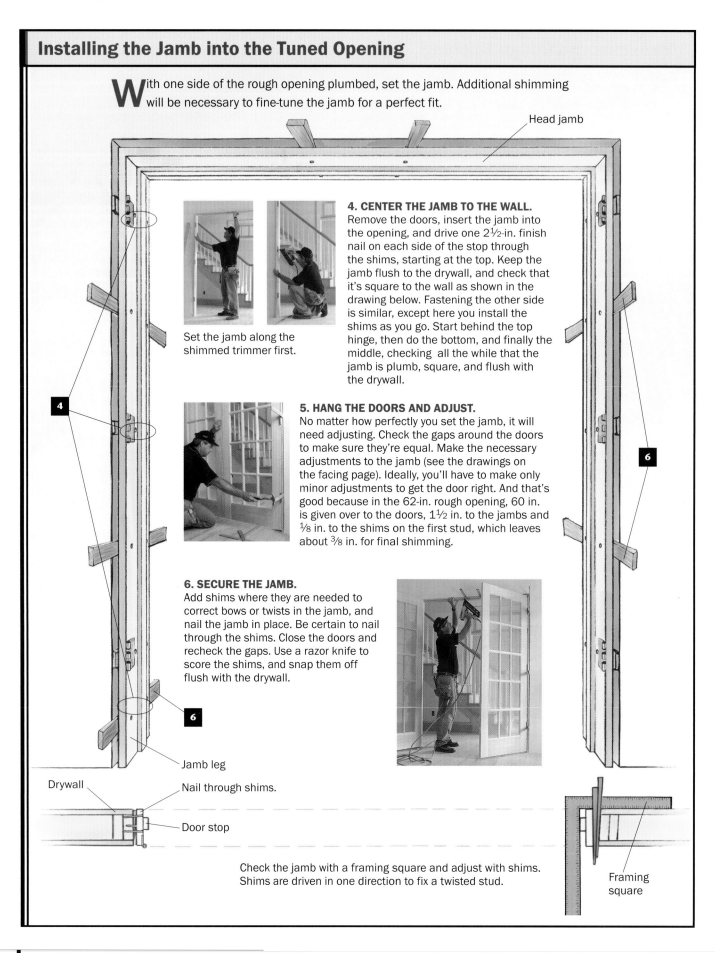

Head jamb

Set the jamb along the shimmed trimmer first.

4

4. CENTER THE JAMB TO THE WALL.
Remove the doors, insert the jamb into the opening, and drive one 2½-in. finish nail on each side of the stop through the shims, starting at the top. Keep the jamb flush to the drywall, and check that it's square to the wall as shown in the drawing below. Fastening the other side is similar, except here you install the shims as you go. Start behind the top hinge, then do the bottom, and finally the middle, checking all the while that the jamb is plumb, square, and flush with the drywall.

5. HANG THE DOORS AND ADJUST.
No matter how perfectly you set the jamb, it will need adjusting. Check the gaps around the doors to make sure they're equal. Make the necessary adjustments to the jamb (see the drawings on the facing page). Ideally, you'll have to make only minor adjustments to get the door right. And that's good because in the 62-in. rough opening, 60 in. is given over to the doors, 1½ in. to the jambs and ⅛ in. to the shims on the first stud, which leaves about ⅜ in. for final shimming.

6. SECURE THE JAMB.
Add shims where they are needed to correct bows or twists in the jamb, and nail the jamb in place. Be certain to nail through the shims. Close the doors and recheck the gaps. Use a razor knife to score the shims, and snap them off flush with the drywall.

6

6

Jamb leg

Drywall

Nail through shims.

Door stop

Check the jamb with a framing square and adjust with shims. Shims are driven in one direction to fix a twisted stud.

Framing square

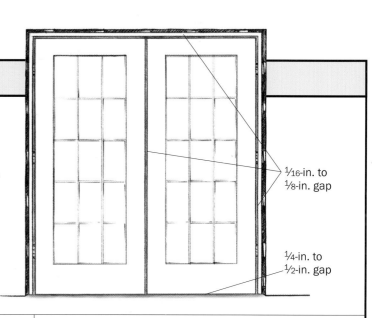

The Ideal Door Installation

French doors should have a nickel-thick gap all the way around. Wood doors shrink and grow with humidity. This gap ensures clearance for the doors to open and close even when swollen with moisture. If you want to be really good, gauge the humidity when you're installing the doors. If they're already swollen, make the gap between them a bit tighter so that it doesn't open objectionably when the wood dries out. If the doors are dry when hung, allow a little extra room for growth. If gaps are uneven, the drawings show how to get them right.

$\frac{1}{16}$-in. to $\frac{1}{8}$-in. gap

$\frac{1}{4}$-in. to $\frac{1}{2}$-in. gap

PROBLEM There's an uneven gap between the door and the head jamb and a wider gap at the bottom between the doors.

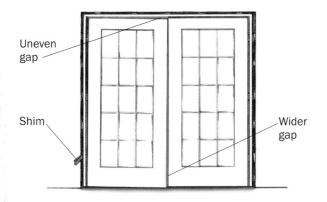

Uneven gap

Shim

Wider gap

SOLUTION Tap in an extra shim behind the bottom hinge, as shown, to even the gaps around the doors.

PROBLEM There's a wider gap between the doors near the head jamb and too little at the bottom.

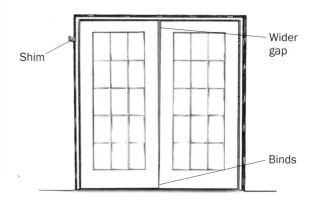

Shim

Wider gap

Binds

SOLUTION Shim behind top hinge, as shown.

PROBLEM There's an even gap between the doors, but they aren't aligned.

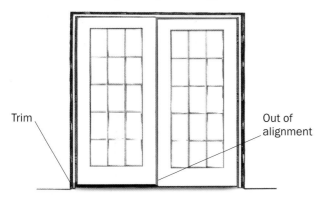

Trim

Out of alignment

SOLUTION One of the jamb legs is too long. With a handsaw, shorten the longer leg by the difference between the two doors. Then pry down on the top of the cut jamb leg. If it doesn't move, cut or pull the nails holding that leg, lower it, and renail.

PROBLEM The doors aren't in plane

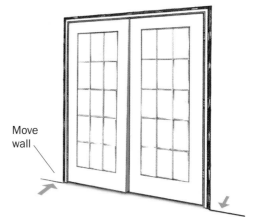

Move wall

SOLUTION Check the walls for plumb, and adjust with a sledge as in the bottom drawing on p. 27. If both walls are plumb, a door is bowed. Replace it, or split the difference by knocking each wall a little out of plumb.

First Aid for Doors

■ SCOTT MCBRIDE

Doors are unlike countertops, fireplace mantels, and many other building components: They're designed to move. We depend on them to open and close smoothly, day after day. When they stick or bind, it's nothing but aggravation.

High humidity is a temporary condition that can swell a door in its frame. But a sticking door also can be the outward sign of something years in the making: a settling foundation, shrinkage in the framing, or hinges that have loosened.

It may seem sensible to plane the latch-side edge of a door where it rubs against the jamb. Nine times out of ten, however, the real problem is on the opposite side: the hinge side. One of the best aids in pinpointing the problem is the gap between the door and the jamb. Ideally, it should be an even 3/32 in. or so on the sides and top and enough to clear the floor easily. Finding where the gap (also called the margin) is either too large or too small can point to the real culprit and suggest a long-lasting solution.

Loose Hinge Screws Cause Binding on the Latch Side

As the screws securing the top hinge loosen due to constant tension, the gap at the hinge side of the door widens, and the gap on the latch side of the door gradually closes until the door starts to bind at the top (see the drawing on the facing page). To identify this problem, open the door slightly and pull upward on the knob while looking at the uppermost hinge. Check for play between the hinge and the jamb and between the hinge and the door. Also, note whether there's any movement in the middle or lower hinges. A loose lower hinge allows the bottom of the door to move toward the hinge jamb, worsening the problem.

Improperly sized pilot holes for hinge screws often lead to trouble. When pilot holes are too large, screw threads can't bite into the wood; when holes are too small, the wood may split. Pilot holes should be the same size as the root diameter of the screw, the part of the shank between threads.

If there are loose hinge screws in either the door or the jamb, open the door as far as it goes and insert shims between the bottom of the door and the floor to take weight off the hinges. One by one, remove the loose screws, drill new pilot holes, and install screws about 1½ in. longer than the originals. There's no point in replacing the screws closest to the hinge barrel on the jamb leaf because they'll probably grab only plaster or drywall (see the right drawing on p. 32). Screws closest to the doorstop, however, should be long enough to penetrate the stud behind the jamb.

If the hinge leaf on a hollow-core door has loosened, longer screws may not work because wooden stiles inside the door are often only 1 in. thick. A longer screw hits only air. On this type of door, try reinserting the screws with a dab of five-minute epoxy on the threads. Keep the door propped up until the glue has set. If that doesn't work, consider relocating the hinges or replacing the door. Screws also may work loose in doors with a solid core of particleboard. In that case, try using long screws—3 in. to 4 in.—and drill the pilot holes slightly smaller than you ordinarily would.

Bent or Improperly Mortised Hinges also Cause Latch-Side Rubbing

When hinges are fastened tightly but the door still binds on the latch side—typically at the top—the problem may be a bent hinge (see the right drawing on p. 32). To adjust the margins at the top of the door, bend the hinge knuckles with an adjustable wrench. First, lift the pin until it engages only the top knuckle. Leave the knuckles on the jamb leaf alone, but use the wrench to bend the knuckles on the door leaf gently. Moving the knuckles toward the lock narrows the margin on the hinge side and widens it on the latch side. If you overshoot the mark, simply reverse the procedure, then reinstall the pin.

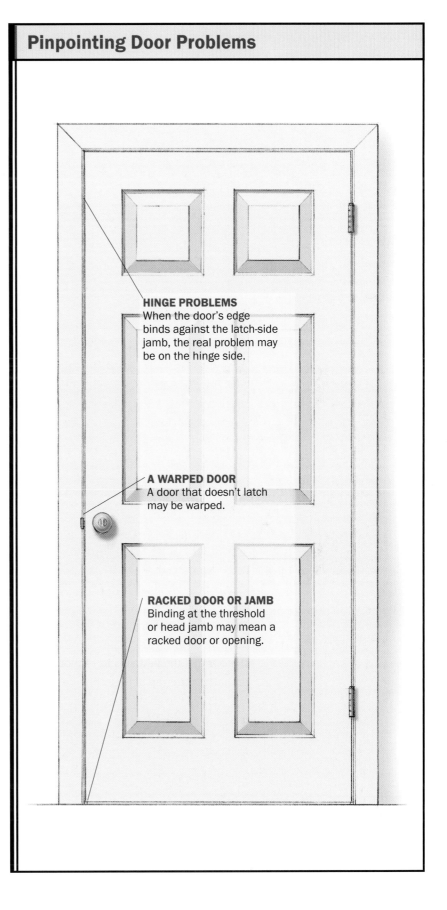

Pinpointing Door Problems

HINGE PROBLEMS
When the door's edge binds against the latch-side jamb, the real problem may be on the hinge side.

A WARPED DOOR
A door that doesn't latch may be warped.

RACKED DOOR OR JAMB
Binding at the threshold or head jamb may mean a racked door or opening.

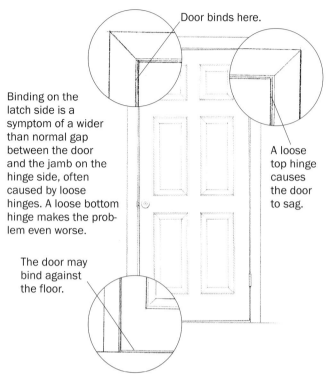

Door binds here.

Binding on the latch side is a symptom of a wider than normal gap between the door and the jamb on the hinge side, often caused by loose hinges. A loose bottom hinge makes the problem even worse.

A loose top hinge causes the door to sag.

The door may bind against the floor.

FOR LATCH-SIDE BINDING, LOOK FOR LOOSE HINGES

To narrow the gap on the hinge side caused by loose hinges, replace the original hinge screws in either the door or the jamb with longer ones, which relieves binding on the latch side of the door. Replacing the outer screw on the jamb leaf may be ineffective, but inner screws should reach the stud that frames the door opening.

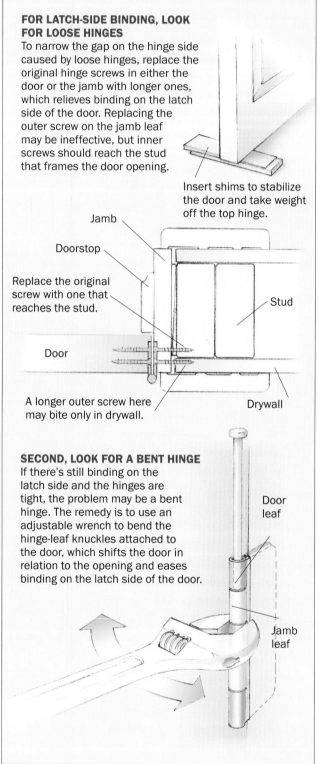

Insert shims to stabilize the door and take weight off the top hinge.

Jamb

Doorstop

Replace the original screw with one that reaches the stud.

Stud

Door

A longer outer screw here may bite only in drywall.

Drywall

SECOND, LOOK FOR A BENT HINGE

If there's still binding on the latch side and the hinges are tight, the problem may be a bent hinge. The remedy is to use an adjustable wrench to bend the hinge-leaf knuckles attached to the door, which shifts the door in relation to the opening and eases binding on the latch side of the door.

Door leaf

Jamb leaf

FOR HINGE-SIDE BINDING

The best way to treat binding on the hinge side is to widen the gap between the door and the hinge jamb by inserting cardboard shims beneath the jamb leaf. After shims have been added and screws retightened, trim excess cardboard with a utility knife.

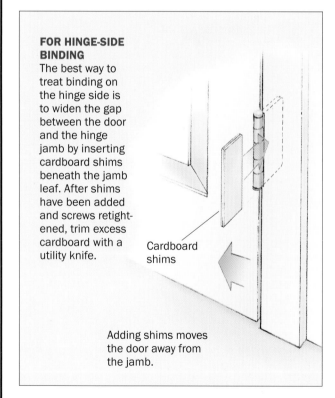

Cardboard shims

Adding shims moves the door away from the jamb.

An alternative to bending hinge knuckles to increase the gap at a hinge is to insert cardboard shims between the hinge leaf and jamb. Most of the time, this adjustment is necessary at the bottom hinge, which is under compression. Widening the gap at the bottom hinge narrows the gap between the door and the head jamb on the latch side of the door (see the bottom left drawing on the facing page). Shimming a hinge also is useful when a hinge gain, or recess, has been cut too deeply and the door binds on the hinge side.

To shim the bottom hinge, open the door and loosen the screws on the jamb leaf a few turns. Cut cardboard strips about ½ in. wide and almost as long as the hinge is tall. Lift the door on the latch side with one hand, which opens a gap between the hinge and the jamb (for heavy doors, use a pry bar). Slip a shim or two into the gap with your other hand until it presses against the hinge screws. Tighten the screws, and test the door's fit. When you have installed the correct number of shims and retightened the screws, trim off any excess with a utility knife.

When a door begins to look like a potato chip—because one or both stiles warp—the latch-side stile will not contact the doorstop evenly. To close the door, a lot of force may be needed to bend the warped stile flat. The same problem crops up when one leg of the door frame doesn't lie in the same plane as the other. There are two solutions. One is to move the position of the stop on the latch-side jamb. The other is to move either the top or bottom hinge away from the door-stop. The door or frame still will be warped, but it will close with less difficulty.

Door or Door Frame Is Racked

Binding at either the head or the sill is a symptom of a racked door or jamb. Foundation settlement or shrinkage in the framing may cause a door frame to rack; old doors usually rack from failed glue joints.

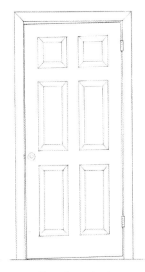

Door frame is racked. Door is racked.

FIT THE DOOR TO THE OPENING
The proper cure for a racked door or opening is to use a pair of dividers to scribe a line on the door along the door's binding head or sill. Cutting along this line yields an even gap.

Use dividers to scribe the door; then trim the top to fit.

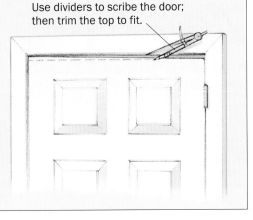

ADJUST THE STRIKE PLATE WHEN THE DOOR WON'T LATCH
When the latch bolt can't fully engage the recess in the strike plate because of racking, the door won't stay shut. Moving the strike plate slightly, or filing the opening, corrects the problem.

Strike plate

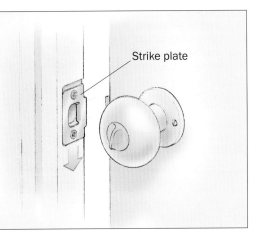

If the door contacts the latch-side stop at the top but not at the bottom (or the other way around) and is difficult to latch, the door is warped, or the frame is twisted.

Warped door

Twisted Frame

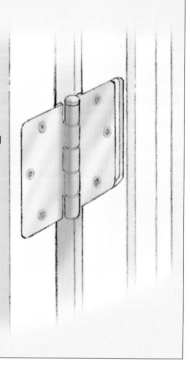

MOVING THE HINGE CAN COMPENSATE FOR WARPING
A door can be coaxed into closing smoothly by shifting either the top or the bottom hinge outward at the jamb.

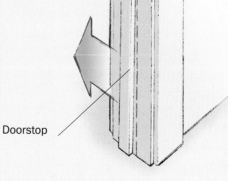

MOVE THE STOP TO COMPENSATE FOR WARPING
If moving the hinge doesn't work, it may be necessary to move the doorstop so that it contacts the entire latch side of the door.

Doorstop

Racking and Swelling May Mean Refitting the Door

Sometimes no amount of hinge adjustment allows a door to close properly. One of two things usually can be blamed: Either the door opening or the door itself has changed shape. The door frame may have racked because the foundation settled or the framing dried unevenly. That's common in old houses. Alternatively, a door may sag as the joints that hold it together loosen over time. This situation is more common with doweled doors than with mortise-and-tenon doors. It may be possible to knock the door apart and reglue it, but it's usually quicker simply to trim the door or to replace it.

Racking causes the door to bind on the latch side, either at the top against the head or at the bottom against the sill. The solution is to trim a tapered piece of wood from the top or bottom of the door. Rather than use a straightedge to lay this out, set a compass to at least ⅛ in. and scribe along the binding head or sill. If the frame or floor wavers, the scribe transfers the line accurately to the door so that the gap remains constant.

After one end of the door has been trimmed, a tapered piece can be added to the other end to make the gap even at the top and bottom. Wet glue can make a tapered filler piece curl at the feather end, so to produce a tight joint, I attach an oversize piece and then trim it to fit after the glue dries.

High humidity can swell a door and cause it to stick in the jamb. Check first to make sure the gap on the hinge side is correct and that hinges are tight. If the hinge-side gap is an even ⅛ in. and the door sticks on the latch side, the door should be removed so that the latch-side edge can be planed to fit. If the entire edge must be planed, the latch has to be removed. After the edge is planed, the latch-plate gain must be deepened.

Also, if you plane down the edge enough, a cylinder lock might end up rubbing on the inside edge of the face bore when you reinstall it. Similarly, in the case of a mortise lock, the knob spindle might rub the sides of the spindle bore. In either case, you need to enlarge the bore slightly with a rasp or router. Don't use a jigsaw for this task; it may chip the wood's surface. Then plane the latch-side edge with a bevel of about 3 degrees so that the inner corner clears the jamb as the door closes. Paint dulls a plane iron immediately, so it's a good idea to scrape or sand off any finish before taking your prized jointer plane out of the toolbox.

Adjusting a Strike Plate

When a door or door frame racks, the latch bolt may no longer line up correctly with the strike plate. Although the door may close smoothly, it refuses to latch. No amount of slamming seems to make it any better.

To fix it, swing the door nearly closed, and mark the jamb where the latch bolt intersects it. Then open the door and check whether the strike plate must be moved up or down. Remove the plate, enlarge the gain with a chisel, and reinstall. Try, however, to move the strike plate at least ¼ in. so that you can drill fresh pilot holes for the plate screws. If you move it less than that, the screws may wander back into the old holes. Use epoxy filler to conceal the newly exposed portion of the gain.

Sometimes the opening in the strike plate is so close in size to the latch bolt that the plate can't be moved ¼ in. In that case, enlarge the opening in the plate. Remove the plate, reshape the opening with a file, and reinstall.

Scott McBride is a contributing editor to Fine Homebuilding.

A Different Approach to Frame-and-Panel Doors

■ GARY STRIEGLER

A good carpenter can make almost any wooden thing that goes into a house. However, I've learned that just because I can make something doesn't necessarily make it profitable or in my client's best interest.

This principle came to mind recently when a client asked me if I could make a couple of frame-and-panel doors with a panel detail that matched the beaded design in some of her cabinets. Doors are typically built in specialty shops, and for good reason. Most frame-and-panel doors are cope-and-stick joined, where the pattern molded inside the rails and stiles holds the panels in place and the ends of the rails are machine-coped to butt to the stiles. Dowels reinforce these joints.

Sometimes, building a door makes sense. This site-built door, with a beaded panel that matches the cabinets, would have cost hundreds of dollars more at a millwork shop.

Two Frames Sandwich an Inner Layer

Hidden pocket screws join the rails and stiles of a pair of ¾-in.-thick frames. A center layer of ¼-in.-thick material overlaps the joints in the frames. Once glued in place, this layer acts much like a tenon to join together the door.

Glass

Molding secures panels.

Rails

Stiles

Molding

Frame

Pocket screws join frame.

Inner layer

Frame

Panel

Decorative molding

Mortise-and-tenon joints are an alternative, but neither method lends itself to small jobs. Cope-and-stick doors call for a shaper and expensive cutters; mortise-and-tenon doors take lots of machines or lots of time.

However, I've used a third method that requires minimal tooling to build doors. Using this method, a front frame and a back frame are glued together around a thin inner layer that acts as tenons to join the stiles and rails of the two frames. Because only a few doors were involved in this project, my client's unusual detailing would have made using a door manufacturer expensive. In this case, my unconventional method made making doors both profitable and in my client's best interest.

Gary Striegler is the principal of Striegler and Associates, a custom-home contractor in Fayetteville, Arkansas.

Begin by Building Two Frames

It's critical to select dimensionally stable, straight, flat wood for the frames. For paint-grade work, the author prefers poplar. Precise rail and stile cuts make a square door, so double-check your saw settings.

Flat doors are built on flat tables. By checking level diagonally from each corner, the author ensures a flat table. Because the door will be glued and clamped on this table, its flatness is critical.

Here's the Cheating Part

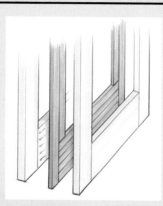

A layer of thin stock glued between the frames effectively creates tenons that lap the stiles. Outer strips that run parallel to the stiles hide the tenon layer's end grain.

Brads keep the splines from sliding on the glue. The inner layer is composed of multiple strips ripped from scrap. As long as enough are used, their width doesn't matter much.

Pocket screws make sturdy frames. A jig (Kreg® Tool Co.; www.kregtool.com; 800-447-8638; $140*) guides the drill that bores holes for screws that join the stiles and rails from behind.

Locking pliers align the rail and stile faces. Screws driven into the bored pockets tighten the stile-to-rail joint in a way that's analogous to toenailing.

An air-powered impact driver speeds clamping. Hex nuts welded to clamp screws accommodate the driver. A few brads keep the frames from sliding out of place.

Marrying the frames. With the inner layer glued and tacked, the second frame is placed atop the first.

A quick pass with a flush-trimming router evens up the edges. Most of the glue squeeze-out had been scraped off to avoid fouling the bit's bearing.

Holding in the Panels

One of the complications of traditional frame-and-panel doors is that the panels are captured by the frame during glue-up. Inadvertently gluing the panels to the frame can cause them to crack. The author avoids this trouble by holding the panels in place with moldings.

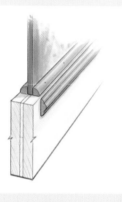

An applied quarter-round molding holds the panels in place. Using a combination square, the author maintains an even reveal as he affixes molding to the frame with a brad gun.

A beaded-plywood panel drops into place. Other panel styles—raised panels or tongue-and-groove boards, for example—can easily be substituted for plywood.

The additional face layer of molding is a southern colonial touch. A flat panel and a simpler molding could give this door a Craftsman look. Whatever the molding, it holds in the upper glass panel as well.

Setting Prehung Doors

■ GARY M. KATZ

In the early 1980s, apartment and condominium construction fueled another building boom in southern California. I remember standing with my brother in the middle of a muddy 380-unit project and staring at receding rows of brand-new two-story town houses. We'd just landed the interior-finish contract, and we both wondered how we'd make a living installing prehung hollow-core doors (see the drawing on the facing page) at $6* each.

But as most carpenters would have done, we jumped into the job feet first. It didn't take us long to learn new tricks for setting prehung doors. By the time we finished that development, my brother and I were convinced that the production techniques we had developed on that job would also work on custom homes, our real bread and butter.

Hanging doors without shimming probably raises a few eyebrows. However, I install only hollow-core 6-ft. 8-in. prehung doors this way. I've installed thousands of doors, and I've never had one settle by itself.

I once returned to an apartment complex to switch the swing of a bathroom door. I guess my crew must have installed the door just before quitting time because the casing on the stop side was not nailed to the wall and the jamb wasn't nailed to

the trimmers at all. But even after being installed this way for two months, the door still fit fine.

Make Certain the Right Doors Are at the Right Openings

Before my crew begins to install doors, I walk through the house and mark a large X on the wall beside each door opening. The X marks the location of the hinges so that the crew will know which way each door swings. Next, we scatter the doors to the correct openings and check each opening to be sure it's framed 2 in. wider than the size of the door.

Most of the prehung doors I install are shipped to the site without attached casing. I always begin installation by nailing the casing to the jamb about every 2 ft. (see the top photo on p. 44) using 1-in., 18-ga. brads, and gluing and bradding the miters together as well. (When setting doors this way, I always use a nail gun. Hand-nailing would negate much of the method's efficiency.) Not only is it easier to set the unit with the casing attached but the casing also firms and straightens the otherwise wiggly

The Parts of a Prehung Door

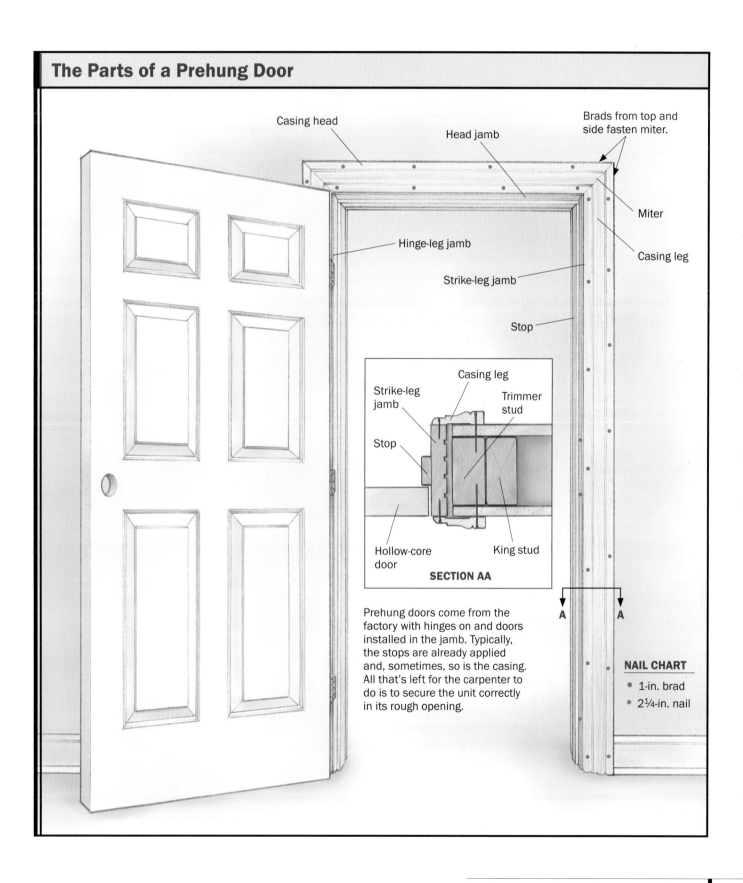

Casing head

Head jamb

Brads from top and side fasten miter.

Miter

Hinge-leg jamb

Casing leg

Strike-leg jamb

Stop

SECTION AA

Casing leg

Strike-leg jamb

Trimmer stud

Stop

King stud

Hollow-core door

A   A

Prehung doors come from the factory with hinges on and doors installed in the jamb. Typically, the stops are already applied and, sometimes, so is the casing. All that's left for the carpenter to do is to secure the unit correctly in its rough opening.

NAIL CHART
- 1-in. brad
- 2¼-in. nail

Casing the prehung unit is the first step. With no drywall irregularities to contend with, perfect casing miters are a snap. The author glues and nails the miters to ensure that they stay perfect.

Set the cased prehung door in the rough opening. So that the unit remains easy to handle, the author will remove the plug or nail that secures jamb to door only after the unit is partially in the opening.

$1\frac{1}{16}$-in.-thick jambs. When I nail the door permanently into the opening, I also shoot some $2\frac{1}{4}$-in., 15-ga. finish nails through the casing into the jamb, especially near the hinges and the floor, to reinforce the brads.

Once the casing is attached, I set the unit partially in the opening (see the bottom photo at left) and pull the plug or the duplex nail that holds the door in the jamb for shipping. Most doors then fall toward the floor, and the head gap between the top of the door and the jamb expands. It might seem that you need three hands to align the jamb and door in the opening, but a prybar well placed on the floor is the only extra help I ever need.

Use Your Foot as a Third Hand

In a perfect world, the houses that I trim would be plumb and level, the doors would all be square, and the jamb legs the same length. That's not how it is, though. What follows is how I hang doors that work well and look good in the often-skewed reality of construction sites.

Although most hollow-core doors aren't too tough to handle, a prybar makes the job easier. I place the prybar under the door (see the left photo on the facing page) a bit closer to the strike side than to the hinge side. If the door has been undercut for carpet, I set a small block of wood on the floor to act as a fulcrum so that the tail end of the prybar is 1 in. or so off the floor.

Stepping lightly on the prybar, just enough to balance the weight of the door, will rack the door back toward the hinge-side jamb. The head gap will close as the door approaches plumb. Also, as I step on the prybar, I rotate the tail end toward the strike jamb. A slight rotation pulls the bottom of the hinge jamb away from the trimmer and helps plumb the door. I find a comfortable stance and apply just enough pressure to hold the door still.

A prybar on the floor controls the door. The author eyes the gap between the head jamb and the door. When the gap is even, he sets the first nail into the wall, just below the miter.

There's more to setting a door than plumb and level. Although setting a door plumb is ideal, it must also look parallel to adjacent walls or trim. A quick check with a tape confirms parallel.

Perfectly Plumb Isn't Always Perfect

If a door is standing alone with no other door or wall nearby, then plumbing the hinge jamb with a good 6-ft. or longer level should determine the door's position in the opening. Perfectly plumb jamb legs and level jamb heads are the best choice.

However, the casing should also be parallel to any adjacent wall or door, which may not be exactly plumb (see the right photo above). I frequently set prehungs slightly out of plumb to achieve even margins with existing walls and trim. So while I'm stepping on the prybar, I pull my tape measure to check the margin between an adjacent door or wall at the top and bottom of the casing.

Also, the head casing must line up with adjacent door and window casings. I check alignment with a level. Occasionally, a jamb must be cut down or shimmed up to align the head casing. The closer adjacent openings are to the door, the more important it is to match them.

Finally, I check the head gap. This margin between the door and the head jamb should be uniform, about the thickness of a nickel (see the sidebar on p. 46). If the floor is out of level, you'll find that the head gap will be too tight or too loose, even if the hinge jamb is plumb. Either jamb leg may have to be shimmed off the floor to even up the gap, but more on that in a minute.

Fixing Uneven Gaps between Door and Jamb

Wide head gap requires correction. Raising the hinge jamb or moving its bottom toward the opening's center will close this gap. Another alternative is to lower the jamb by trimming the bottom of the strike jamb.

Even lightweight hollow-core doors can cause hinge deflection. Notice that the gap between door and jamb is larger above and below the hinge. Raising the door with a prybar and nailing the casing to the wall behind the hinge corrects this problem.

The Right Nailing Sequence Is Crucial

I always place the first nail (I use 15-ga., 2¼-in. pneumatic nails) through the casing and into the wall about 3 in. below the miter on the hinge side (see the left photo on p. 45). Before driving a second nail, I check the head gap again.

If I have the hinge jamb plumb to my liking, a head gap that's too big near the strike jamb (see the top photo at left) means I'll have to shim under the hinge jamb. With only one nail holding it, the jamb can still be easily shifted using a prybar. I place the prybar beneath the door on the hinge side and raise the door and jamb straight up until the head gap is uniform. Once I'm satisfied with the head gap, I shoot the second nail through the casing about 2 in. below the bottom hinge. The nails through the casing will hold the door until I shim between the jamb and the floor. This shim keeps the door from settling and cracking open the miter.

After the first nail, if the head gap is too small, then the floor is out of level in the opposite direction. A shim under the strike jamb cures this problem.

If the floor is level but the head gap is too big anyway, the door is racked in the jamb. I can move the bottom of the hinge jamb inward and close the gap by slightly lifting the door with a prybar, then rotating the prybar. To open the gap, I simply tap the bottom of the hinge jamb toward the trimmer (the inner studs in the rough opening) with a block of wood and a hammer.

After securing the door, I step back a little and take a long look at the head gap and the margins between the casing and the adjacent walls or doors. The two nails I've installed will hold the unit still, but I can still move the jamb easily with a prybar.

Before shooting another nail, I again check the head gap. If it's still too tight, I lift the strike jamb and make sure there's enough wiggle room between the head jamb and the header so that I can correct the gap later. But I don't nail the casing on the strike jamb just yet.

The Third Nail Is the Most Important

The weight of a door always pulls down on the top hinge and often causes the jamb to deflect. Jamb deflection at the top hinge, or tweaking, as we call it, is usually a problem that occurs on heavier solid-core doors, but tweaking can cause problems with hollow-core doors, too. Deflection at the top hinge causes a wide gap between the door and the jamb above and below the top hinge (see the bottom photo on the facing page). And if the hinge gap is too big, you can bet the strike gap will be too tight. Here's how I quickly correct jamb deflection.

With the jamb secured by the first two nails through the casing and with the door closed, I place a prybar under the strike edge of the door and step on it lightly. I apply enough pressure to take the weight of the door off the jamb and to force the jamb and the top hinge back toward the trimmer. Before I place the third nail, I like to see a slightly tight gap between the door and the jamb above the top hinge. The gap between the top of the door and the strike jamb should conversely be slightly large. After the third nail is driven—through the casing and into the trimmer behind the top hinge—the door will settle slightly, and the gaps will be perfect. Then I shoot a fourth nail nearby, just to be sure the gaps stay perfect.

The remainder of the hinge-side casing can now be fastened to the wall. I use about one nail per foot, with an extra nail or two behind each hinge. Next, I drive a nail through the head casing above the strike jamb, about 3 in. away from the miter. Then I tack the strike-side casing to the wall about every 2 ft., keeping the door-to-jamb margin about the thickness of a nickel.

Correcting Cross-legged Jambs

Before attaching the casing to the opposite side of the unit, I straighten any cross-legged jambs. If the jamb is cross-legged, the door won't lie flat against the door stop on the strike side. Sometimes the top of the door will hit the stop, but the bottom won't, which is easy to fix: Just tap the bottom of the strike jamb toward the door with a block of wood and a hammer.

I always adjust for cross-legged jambs at the bottom of the jamb (see the photo below), not at the top. This adjustment keeps the jamb head flush with the drywall so that joining the casing miters on the stop side of the door is easier.

Correcting cross-legged jambs with a boot and tap. The fix when the door doesn't hit the top of the strike-side stop is pushing in on the bottom of the hinge jamb. If the door doesn't hit the bottom of the stop, simply moving the strike-jamb bottom toward the door is the cure.

Shimming Solid-Core Doors

Shopmade sled makes cutting shims fast and safe. A sled also serves as a template to cut each shim exactly the same size. The author stops cutting when the block reaches 6 in. in length.

Although I don't shim hollow-core doors, I do shim all solid-core doors, as well as any door that's more than 6 ft. 8 in. tall. Shims should be installed behind every hinge, and there should be at least three sets of shims on the strike side, especially behind the strike plate.

I cut my own end-grain shims from 2x6 scrap on my tablesaw. Although it sounds like a lot of work, it's worth every minute (see the photo above). These shims are all 5½ in. long, ¼ in. thick at the butt end and sharp at the point end. I cut them cross-grain so that they'll snap off easily. Because they're only ¼ in. thick, I can slip one behind most prehung jambs, butt end first, then follow it up with the point of another shim. When they are stacked tightly atop one another, these perfectly uniform shims quickly adjust to fill any odd-size gap between a twisted trimmer and the back of a flat jamb. If space is tight, I use only one shim (see the photos at right). I shoot a nail or two beneath the shims to hold them in place, but I never nail through the shims. It seems that every time I nail through a shim I have to move it later, which is nearly impossible.

Along with shims, I also use screws to secure solid-core door jambs. Heavy doors always cause jamb deflection, and finish nails don't have enough strength to secure the weight. I replace one screw in each hinge with a long screw that reaches through the jamb and into the trimmer. Often I replace two

Solid-core doors get shimmed and screwed. Homemade end-grain shims that snap off cleanly go behind each hinge and behind the strike plate of solid-core doors. A 2½-in. screw through the hinge ensures that the door won't sag.

screws in the top hinge. I tighten the screws carefully because too much torque will cause a belly in the jamb and ruin the fit of the door. If I don't have the right size screw, I remove the hinge from the jamb and countersink a screw behind the hinge, then reattach the hinge to the jamb.

If the bottom of the door touches the strike-side stop but the top doesn't, then tapping the bottom of the hinge jamb toward the door is the fix. I press against the door or the jamb leg with my shoe, then smack the jamb leg. Once the door is flat against the stop, I nail through the face of the jamb a few inches from the floor to hold the jamb in place.

After I've corrected any cross-legged jambs, I install the casing on the other side of the opening, nailing only into the jamb (see the photo above). Then I check the fit of the door once more before nailing the casing to the wall. If necessary, the jamb can still be adjusted minutely with a hammer, a block of wood and a few light taps. Once I'm satisfied with the fit, I nail off the casing on the hinge side with a nail about every 12 in. I also place one nail above the strike and one below. In addition, I drive a nail through the casing about 2 in. above the floor. This way, if the baseboard is cut and installed too tight, it won't push the jamb and ruin the fit of the door. I also shoot a nail through the jamb, above and below each hinge, to prevent the door from settling (see the photo at right). Finally, because I never shim hollow-core prehung doors, I replace one of the short hinge screws in the top hinge with a long screw that reaches through the jamb to the trimmer. I tighten that screw only enough to seat it snugly.

*Note prices are from 1998.

Gary M. Katz is a carpenter in Reseda, California, and the author of The Doorhanger's Handbook (The Taunton Press, 1998).

Three Ways to Weatherstrip a Door

■ GARY M. KATZ

Weatherproofing exterior doors isn't important. It's critical. When wind-driven water finds its way inside a house, it can seep into and stain wood floors, delaminate the plywood underneath the floor, and get into vinyl and laminate flooring. Just as bad—or worse—are the invisible air leaks around doors. A weak seal between door and jamb can cost plenty in escaping energy.

This is why weatherstripping is so important. Although weatherstripping an exterior door won't make it seal like a refrigerator, these gasketlike strips will help keep wind and water where they belong—outside. As usual in the building industry, though, there seems to be a dizzying array of weatherstripping products, at least at first glance. But the subject is fairly black and white—and not just because there are only a few colors to choose from.

I use just three common types of weatherstripping (see the photos on the facing page). All three are easy to install and are usually available at good hardware stores. Most important, all three keep the elements at bay, unlike some of the cheaper stick-on varieties. Unfortunately, no single product is perfect for every door in every home, so knowing the difference makes it easier to choose the right product for your door.

Bronze Will Beat Back a Gale

Bronze is the most durable weatherstripping material, and "cushion bronze" or "V-bronze"—a thin strip of bronze folded lengthwise into a *V* and squeezed between the door and jamb—is the best way to get a tight seal. V-bronze—especially when combined with another seal, such as silicone—stops 99 percent of the water that charges a door. Whether you are remodeling or weatherstripping a new door, V-bronze is hard to beat.

Every miracle cure has side effects, and V-bronze is no exception (see the sidebar on p. 52). Some people don't like its traditional look, and V-bronze can be time consuming and finicky to attach to a door opening. There are lots of little brass nails to drive, you need a separate strip at the lockset, and the stuff is hard to paint around once installed.

To a lot of people, bronze is simply old-fashioned and ineffective compared with other seals. But the bronze they are probably thinking of is "spring bronze," which is far less adept at stopping water than V-bronze. Spring bronze is a flat strip of metal crimped slightly at one edge so that it will contact the door when it closes. The problem with spring bronze is that over time, it loses its spring and flattens out. With V-bronze, weather and light penetration are not a problem.

Rigid-Jamb Weatherstripping Is Popular for Old Doors

Rigid-jamb weatherstripping (also known as "jamb-up" and "adjustable-jamb" weatherstripping) has been widely used since the 1950s and is still installed in many new houses (see the sidebar on p. 54). It's popular among remodelers, especially when the existing door jambs are not being replaced. This type of weatherstripping is screwed to the outside of the door, making it easy to install on old doors.

Another plus is that rigid-jamb weatherstripping—when installed with screws—is adjustable. The screw holes in the metal retainer are slotted so that the bulb can be brought closer to or pulled farther from the door. When you're buying rigid-jamb weatherstripping, be sure to look at the fasteners. If the package includes nails, put it back—it won't be adjustable.

Bronze weathers well. V-bronze is an improvement over flat bronze weatherstripping. It gets squeezed between the door and the jamb, blocking wind and water.

Rigid-jamb seals from the outside. Fastened to the weather side of the door, rigid-jamb weatherstripping is adjustable and easy to install on old jambs.

Kerf-in is the latest twist. Pressed into a thin kerf, or slot, in the jamb, kerf-in vinyl or silicone is often found in new construction.

Installing V-Bronze Weatherstripping

V-bronze combined with a kerf-in silicone seal, as shown in these photos, is perhaps the best defense against wind and water. I put V-bronze weatherstripping on openings that are battered by the weather, and then, ironically, I have to make all the gaps around the door larger—$3/16$ in. instead of the usual $1/8$ in. It helps to bevel the top of a door, which reduces friction and prevents moisture from oxidizing into a green mess.

Installing V-bronze is simple: Start by cutting the head piece to fit between the door rabbets. Trim the flap on each end at a slight angle (3 degrees to 5 degrees) so that the flap won't drag after the legs are installed. Place the bronze flush to the doorstop, and nail the head every 3 in., using a punch to set the nails to avoid marring the jamb.

Install the legs (sides) next, but this time, hold the leg back from the stop $1/4$ in. so that the leg flaps won't interfere with the head flaps (see photo 1). (Offsetting the leg and the head also improves the seal at the top

1

Miter V-bronze in the corners. To avoid overlap, the V-bronze flaps are cut at 45-degree angles in the corners. The strips on the side jambs are placed $1/4$ in. away from the stop. Strips of V-bronze are nailed every 3 in.

Spring bronze (top) and V-bronze (bottom) by Pemko (800-283-9988). V-bronze (middle) by Macklanburg-Duncan® (800-654-8454).

of the door.) Don't cut the flap too tight at the threshold, though, or it will bind. You can run the V-bronze over the hinge plates, but you'll have to use a narrower strip around the strike plates for dead bolts and latches (see photo 2).

The bottom corners of a door are the weak spot of any weatherstripping system. To ensure a complete seal at the bottom of the door, nail a corner pad at each end of the threshold (see photo 3). Corner pads are available in black and white and cost only a few cents, and they can be used with all types of weatherstripping.

Adjusting V-bronze is easy. Slide a nail set or punch inside the V-shaped flap, and bend the flap until it contacts the door (see photo 4). If the flap bends too much, press it down with the heel of the punch. I rub paraffin wax on the bronze, which helps stop the metal from talking (see photo 5).

Leave room for the lockset. Strike plates for a dead bolt and latch require narrow V-bronze. Be sure to cut it long for plenty of overlap, and set the nails carefully to avoid marring the bright surface.

Corner pads complete the seal. Corner pads are the best insurance against light and air penetration at the bottom of a door.

Waxed and ready to fight the weather. Paraffin wax silences the strip and ensures smooth door operation.

Use a nail set to adjust the strip. For large gaps, sliding a nail set into the crease will force out the flap. To press it back in again, slide the heel of the nail set against the flap.

Installing Rigid-Jamb Weatherstripping

With a hacksaw or high-rpm circular saw, cut the head first to fit tightly across the jamb (see photo 1). Then shut the door, throw the dead bolt, and press the weatherstripping against the door until the vinyl or silicone bulb touches. Drive one screw into each end, and move on to the legs. It doesn't matter which leg of the jamb is weatherstripped first. Measure from the head to the threshold, and leave enough to scribe the bottom of the weath-

erstripping to a sloped threshold (see photo 2). Before installing the legs, crimp the aluminum over the bulb at both ends so that the bulb won't slide around (see photo 3).

To fasten the legs, press the bulb lightly against the door, and drive one screw at each end and one in the middle (see photo 4). Close the door, and check the lock for smooth operation before inserting more screws.

Rigid-jamb weatherstripping is widely available. Top and bottom are by Macklanburg-Duncan; middle is by Pemko.

1

Cut rigid-jamb weatherstripping with a high-rpm circular saw. A carbide-tipped blade makes short work of the job. A hacksaw works, too, but not tin snips—they leave an ugly scar on the metal.

Most weatherstripping manufacturers offer rigid-jamb weatherstripping with either a vinyl or a silicone bulb seal, and it is important to make the distinction clear. A vinyl bulb does not have much spring. Unless the vinyl bulb is installed just right—not too close to the door but tight enough to seal—it will pinch on the hinges as the door swings closed. On the lockset side, the vinyl bulb may interfere with the action of the door latch if it is installed too tightly.

Silicone, on the other hand, can be installed closer to the door, producing a tighter seal. Unlike vinyl, silicone doesn't harden over time, and it remembers its original, elastic shape. Another benefit of silicone is that paint doesn't stick to it, at least not for long. All these features are welcome in a product exposed to weather and, every few years, to a paintbrush. The big drawback is that silicone is almost twice as expensive as vinyl, adding about $10* per opening.

Rigid-jamb weatherstripping is available for metal jambs, too. I use one that comes with two-sided tape on the back. Only a few predrilled slotted holes are machined into a length of this material (instead of one every 8 in. to 10 in. as in standard rigid jamb), and self-tapping sheet-metal screws are included, rather than wood screws.

2

Scribe the legs to match the threshold. Weatherstripping on the side jambs usually lands on the sloped portion of the threshold, which means you will need to scribe the pieces to get a tight fit.

3

Crimp the ends to freeze the bulb. The vinyl or silicone bulb—the part that actually seals the door—will slide unless the metal is crimped at the ends.

4

Use screws, not nails. Rigid-jamb weatherstripping is adjustable. Drive screws at the top, middle, and bottom; then push the strip in to meet the door before tightening.

Kerf-in Weatherstripping Is Now the Standard for the Industry

Kerf-in weatherstripping is the most common seal you will find on new doors because it works and because it is easy to install. Kerf-in weatherstripping comes in many shapes, sizes, and colors, but they all work the same way: The seal, made of silicone or foam, has a flat fin that holds the seal in a kerf between the stop and the jamb, locking it in place.

I use two types of kerf-in weatherstripping: silicone bead and foam. Silicone bead is a good choice for retrofitting an existing jamb because it compresses almost completely when the door is shut, requiring no additional room (you don't have to increase the depth of the stop).

The problem with silicone bead is not the installation so much as its unreliability at stopping wind and water year after year. I recommend it only for doors that are somewhat protected from the weather. I also encounter another problem with white silicone bead: Because it's translucent, people sometimes glimpse daylight between the

Kerfing Jambs for Silicone and Vinyl

Installing kerf-in foam weather stripping is hard only on your fingertips. Cut the head first, square at each end; then cut the legs with a 45-degree angle at the top so that they cope over the head. The bottoms of the legs should follow the threshold.

I buy my jambs precut and kerfed for foam weatherstipping (see photo 1), but sometimes I have to kerf one or two by myself. I use my tablesaw with a finger board, positioning the fence so that the blade clears the face of the jamb by ⅛ in. (A thin-kerf blade works best.) Adding a slight

angle, about 2 degrees to 3 degrees, minmizes the risk of marring the jamb. Your can also buy a router bit that cuts the kerf and extends the rabbet ⅜ in. for products such as Q-LON®. (Bosch manufactures a flush-cutting sawblade that mounts into a router for kerfing jambs.)

It's nearly impossible to use foam in old doors without performing major jamb surgery. Fortunately, another kerf-in material—silicone bead—makes retrofitting old doors a breeze. I often use silicone corner tube seal (see photo 2). Both the weatherstripping and a special

router base for retrofitting old doorways are available from Resource Conservation Technology (410-366-1146).

The kerfing tool, which attaches to a laminate trimmer has a base angled at 45 degrees to fit in the corner between the stop and the jamb (see photo 3). A bit cuts the angled kerf, and the weatherstripping is pressed into the slot (see photos 4 and 5).

To kerf a jamb, rest the butt of the router base 12 in. to 16 in. from the end of the jamb; then slowly plunge the head of the router into

Kerf cut with tablesaw.

Q-LON vinyl-coated foam, by Schlegel® (800-586-0354; in New York State, 800-462-1727).

1

Kerf cut with router.

Silicone tube seal by Resource Conservation Technology.

2

door and the jamb. One way around this problem is to use a darker color.

Like most weatherstripping products, silicone bead comes in a variety of sizes. I've often used three different sizes on warped doors. Each size fits perfectly inside the next larger diameter, so you can produce a nearly seamless bead. Silicone bead is also perfect for

arched doors. With a laminate-trimmer kerfing tool, you can follow almost any radius or ellipse, and so will the silicone (see the sidebar above).

The other kerf-in product I use—Q-LON—is an S-shaped foam seal. Like silicone bead, kerf-in foam is held inside a thin kerf at the corner where the doorstop meets the rabbet.

the corner between jamb and doorstep. (The angled base makes it easy to hold the tool properly.) Push slowly until the nose of the tool reaches the corner. Then remove the tool, return to the starting point, and finish the rest of the kerf in the opposite direction.

3

A laminate trimmer for retrofitting weatherstripping Designed for installing kerf-in weatherstripping on existing doors, this kerfing tool has a 45-degree angled base that slides in the door rabbet and cuts an angled groove for silicone-bead weatherstripping.

4

5

Just press to fit. Silicone bead and other kerf-in weatherstripping is easy to install. Just cut the corners at a 45-degree angle, and press the flat fin into the kerf.

Cut the groove toward the corners. Plunge the router into the corner of the rabbet, and move it slowly toward the top and bottom corners of the jambs. A vacuum hose sucks up stray sawdust.

Unlike silicone, products like Q-LON take up a lot of room between the door and the stop, making them a bad choice for retrofitting old doors without performing major surgery on the jambs.

I prefer foam over silicone bead because it works well, it's easy to install on new doors, and it rarely interferes with the door's operation. The biggest problem with foam prod-

ucts, however, is that they are clearly visible between the stop and the door, a look some people find distracting.

*Note prices are from 1998.

Gary M. Katz *is a carpenter in Reseda, California, and the author of* The Door Hanger's Handbook *(The Taunton Press, 1998).*

Installing Bifold Doors

■ JIM BRITTON

1

Start by assembling the jamb. First, the author spreads out the jamb parts in front of the closet. Then he uses a pneumatic stapler to anchor the side jamb to the head jamb.

2

A 1x strip hides the door track. Once the jambs are assembled, the author attaches a 1x2 to the inside of the head jamb. The door track tucks against the backside of this strip.

3

Next, nail the casings to the jamb stock. Leaving a $3/16$-in. reveal around the inside edges of the jambs, the author readies the jamb assembly by nailing on the casings.

If you work as a trim carpenter long enough, sooner or later you'll come to the realization that prefabricating components on a bench makes it easier to put them on the wall. I put this approach to work in all my trim-carpentry tasks. But in the case of installing bifold doors—the ubiquitous accordion-style panels that conceal many an American closet—the workbench is the floor in front of the closet. The job starts with the jambs.

Unlike prehung doors, which are hinged to their jambs when they leave the factory, bifold doors are typically shipped without the jambs. Instead, bifold doors are hinged to one another and packed in a cardboard box. The box also contains a bag full of hardware for hanging the doors. The doors illustrated here, for example, included the 2400 series Bi-Fold Door Hardware from Stanley®. Detailed instructions for adjusting the hardware accompany the doors.

I typically purchase bifold doors from the same shop that supplies my passage doors. Along with the doors, I have the shop send along finger-jointed pine jamb kits for the doors. I prefer pine because nails driven into pine—unlike medium-density fiberboard (MDF), the other jamb-material option—don't leave telltale dimples that need sanding.

4

Shims elevate the jambs. With a spirit level long enough to span the rough opening, the author assesses the floor for level and places shims accordingly next to the trimmer studs. The shims, which are at least ⅜ in. thick, lift the jambs enough to accommodate the carpet.

5

Lift the pretrimmed jamb into its opening. With the bottoms of the side jambs sitting on their shims to ensure a level head jamb, the author slides the jamb assembly into the rough opening. Affixing it to the rough-opening frame starts from the top down.

6

Center the head jamb. Next, the author slides the assembly from right to left, and marks the positions with a pencil. Splitting the difference centers the jamb. One nail through the casing into the header maintains alignment at this stage.

7

Plumb the side jamb. The author uses the 6-ft. level to check the side jamb for plumb, moving the bottom of the jamb toward or away from the trimmer until the bubble is centered. Once he's got it right, he affixes the casing to the trimmer with a nail near the bottom of the jamb.

8

Shim the jamb, and nail it home. Once the jamb has been plumbed, it can be permanently affixed to the trimmer. The author uses a 15-ga. nailer, driving the fasteners through shims to keep the jamb from deflecting toward the framing as the nails slam home.

9

Now go to the other side. The bottom of the opposite jamb is located with a tape measure. The distance between the jambs at the top should be repeated here. Double-check for square by measuring the diagonals from casing corners to jamb bottoms.

Rough openings should be sized in a manner similar to those for passage doors by adding 2 in. to the nominal dimension of the doors. For example, a 5-ft. 0-in. bifold requires a 62-in.-wide rough opening. That leaves enough room for the jambs (two at ⅝ in. each) plus some wiggle room for plumbing the jambs. I frame my rough openings to be 82½ in. high from the subfloor. That's a standard 81-in. trimmer atop a 2x plate. Sharp-eyed carpenters will note that even though they are called 6-ft. 8-in. doors, bifold doors are really 6 ft. 7 in. tall. The missing inch allows room for the track at the top of the doors.

The head casing gets nailed on last. The author takes a slight bow out of the head casing by flattening it against the level as he nails the casing to the header.

Screw the track to the head jamb. The door track fits flush against the 1x2 nailed to the inside of the head jamb. If the screws reach the header, be sure to shim the jamb to keep it from deflecting.

The doors swing on pins (13, 14). At the top, each door has a spring-loaded pivot pin (top) that slides in the door track. At the bottom, the door closest to the jamb has an adjustable pin that fits into the jamb bracket (bottom).

Align the jamb brackets with the door track. At the base of each side jamb, an L-shaped bracket supports a pivot pin mounted in the bottom of the pivot door. The serrations in the slot capture the star-shaped pivot pin at the bottom of the door, holding it at the desired distance from the jamb. The bracket sits atop a ³⁄₈-in.-thick plywood block, which keeps the bracket from being buried by the carpeting. A pencil mark on the side jamb notes the centerline of the door track above.

The jamb kits often include 1x1 moldings that are meant to conceal the edges of the doors around the sides and the door track. I think they're ugly. These clunky 1x1s give a tacked-on look to the trim that isn't in keeping with the look of the passage doors. So I leave out the 1x1s, preferring instead a detail that I learned from an ace finish carpenter back in the 1970s. As shown in photos 2 and 11, I add a 1x2 to the head jamb, and then conceal most of it with the same trim that cases the passage doors. I don't use any stops along the sides of the doors because the doors can easily be adjusted to maintain an even gap between their stiles and the jambs when the side jambs are aligned correctly.

Install the doors from the top. Insert the top pivot pins into their slots, and push up to compress the springs. This makes room for the lower pivot to clear the jamb bracket as its pin is located in the serrated slot.

Bifold doors swing on pins instead of on the leaf hinges common to passage doors. The pins fit into predrilled holes in the top and bottom of the doors. With this system, most of the loads exerted by the doors are delivered to the pivot brackets at the bottoms of the jambs. So don't worry about heavy structural nailing through the jambs to keep the doors from sagging. You'll note in the photos that I put blocks under the pivot brackets to keep them from being buried by carpeting. If the floor is to be hardwood, leave out the blocks and install the doors after the hardwood is in place.

Hardware varies a bit from brand to brand, but the principles are the same. The door

Ready for knobs. The door closest to the jamb in a pair of bifold doors is called the pivot door. Its mate is called a guide door. You'll get the best leverage for opening and closing the doors by affixing the knobs to the pivot doors.

Aligners keep the guide doors flush with one another. Metal tabs called aligners are installed about 12 in. above the floor on the backside of the bifold doors. As the doors are brought together, the aligners engage one another to snap the doors closed.

closest to the jamb is the pivot door. Its mate is the guide door. The pivot bracket at the bottom of the jamb is fixed, but the pin can be moved along its serrated slot to fine-tune the pivot door's distance from the jamb. The pin at the top of the pivot door fits into a bracket in the door track that can be adjusted with a set screw. The pin in the guide door fits into a sliding, spring-loaded guide that snugs against the other pair of doors, holding them tightly together when closed.

Jim Britton is a carpenter and general contractor in Jacksonville, Oregon.

Installing
Sliding Doors

■ GARY M. KATZ

I recently got a call from a homeowner who wanted me to come out and adjust a sliding door that wasn't working right. It sounded like a small job, so I figured that my toolbox and cordless drill were all the tools I'd need. I was wrong.

Right away, I had trouble unlocking the sliding door. The homeowner explained that the only way she could get the door to latch was by slamming it as hard as she could against the jamb. With the unlocked door close to the jamb, I could see part of the problem. The door was touching the jamb at the top but was more than ¼ in. away from the jamb at the bottom. I said to myself, Hey, this'll be a snap. I'll just raise the front wheel on the door, and the lady will think I'm a genius.

But when I slid the door back to get at the wheel-adjustment screw, the back of the door was rubbing so badly on the head jamb that the slider would open only halfway. I said to myself, Hey, this'll be a snap. I'll just lower the back wheel, and the lady will think I'm a genius. But the rear wheels were already set as low as they could go. That's when I noticed that the head jamb was pushed way up in the center.

Then I got down on my hands and knees, sighted down the sill and saw the real problem. The oak sill looked like a foothill in the San Gabriel Mountains. An improperly set sill is a classic, common mistake made while installing prefit sliding-door units. By following just a few a simple steps, you'll be able to avoid that mistake, and a few others, too.

Start at the bottom.
The first step in installing a slider is leveling the threshold. Lay a long level on the rough opening, and shim the threshold up to the proper level.

Make Sure the Door Is Going to Fit

I admit it: I've been embarrassed by removing an old door before realizing that the new unit wasn't going to fit. So now I always measure the opening or, on a remodel, I measure what will become the opening before the door is ordered.

I like to have the rough opening about ½ in. larger in width and height, though some slider manufacturers call for rough openings a little bigger, in some cases 1 in. wider and taller than the unit dimensions. Sometimes the extra space is more than necessary, and sometimes it's not nearly enough if the floor of the opening is out of level or has a big hump in it.

If I'm working on a concrete slab that is grossly out of level or if the threshold has a terrible high spot, I know I'm going to need more head clearance. I look for these problems before assembling the frame by checking the threshold with a long level. If there is an old door in the opening, I check the floor just inside the threshold for obvious humps or for an out-of-level floor. It's also a good idea to give the jambs a quick check. If they're out of plumb, I may need to make the rough opening a little wider.

Although the wood sills on most sliders are back-primed by the manufacturer, some still need to be back-primed or sealed by the installer. If the sill isn't sealed properly, it will warp and twist. If the sill hasn't been thoroughly primed, I start back-priming as soon as I'm sure that the slider is the right size and that it won't be going back to the store. If possible, I start back-priming before removing the old unit so that I can get at least two good coats of exterior primer on the sill before it's time to assemble the frame. If the whole frame is wood, I also make sure that the bottoms of the side jambs are back-primed to keep the end grain from soaking up moisture.

Level the Sill in the Rough Opening

I begin prepping the opening by cleaning the threshold. Then I lay down the longest level I have that will fit between the jambs (see the photo on p. 64). A short level placed on top of a straight board also works well. I shim up the low end until it's perfectly level; then I fill in the gaps between the level and the floor with additional shims placed about every 12 in. On concrete slabs I hold each shim in place with a blob of silicone adhe-

A paper drain pan. Special waterproof-paper flashing is layered in beds of silicone to form a drain pan under the slider.

sive. On wood floors I nail the shims down so that they won't move when I slide the frame in and out during the dry fit. I always double-check the header height from the top of the shims. If there's not enough room, I'll have to get a shorter slider. Next, I make sure the trimmer studs that flank the opening are plumb. I measure the width of the opening, and I add furring to the trimmers if the opening is too wide.

The next step is flashing the threshold to keep water from coming in under the door. If I've had an aluminum drain pan made for me, I press it into a bed of silicone right over the shims, making sure that corners and seams are well sealed.

If no aluminum drain pan is available (which is the case on virtually every remodeling job where I install a slider), I make the pan out of layers of Moistop® (Fortifiber Corp., 1001 Tahoe Blvd., Incline Village, NV 89451; 800-773-4777), a fiber-reinforced waterproof-paper flashing with a polyethylene coating on both sides. Moistop comes in 6-in.-wide rolls. I cut the first layer of paper flashing about 12 in. longer than the opening so that ends extend up the jambs, and I install that layer in a bed of silicone over the shims (see the photo on the facing page). I let a few inches of the paper flashing lap over the outside edge of the sill. Staples keep the flashing in place while the silicone adhesive is curing.

I cut a second layer the same length and bed it in silicone over the first layer, only this time I let the excess paper flashing extend into the room. If there is hardwood flooring or a subfloor that the sliding door will fit against, I wrap the excess flashing up the edge of the flooring to create a dam. If there is no flooring or subfloor, I leave the excess flap until after the door is installed, and then I staple it to the inside edge of the slider threshold to form the dam. Finally, I caulk a short piece of paper flashing into each corner, making sure that the stacked-up layers provide complete coverage.

Drill anchor holes during the dry fit. After the frame has been tested in the opening, anchor holes are drilled through holes in the sill with a masonry bit.

A Dry Fit Locates the Anchor Positions

The frames for most sliders—no matter whether they're wood, metal, or vinyl—have to be assembled on site. I lay all the pieces on a flat, open area with the outside facing up, and I screw the corners together after sealing them with silicone.

Before bedding the frame on top of the drain pan, I test the assembled frame in the opening to be absolutely sure that the door is going to fit right. If screws and concrete anchors are being used to secure the sill, a dry run is the best way to locate the anchors.

After centering the frame in the opening, I make sure that there's ample room to plumb the side jambs. If I'm installing the door over concrete, I mark both ends of the sill so that I can put it in the exact same position when I install it for good. For aluminum or vinyl sills, I run a masonry bit through the factory-drilled holes, drilling into the concrete for the plastic anchors (see the photo above). I locate concrete

Slider frame is bedded in caulk. Caulking is applied around the framed opening, and the nailing flanges on the side jambs are pressed into the caulk and fastened temporarily until the jambs are plumbed.

anchors the same way for sills on wood sliders, only first I counterbore the holes for wood plugs, which I install later to cover the screw heads.

After all the anchors are located, I remove the frame from the opening, sweep out the dust and dirt, and then insert the plastic concrete anchors. Before slipping the frame back into the opening, I lay down another bed of silicone caulking on top of the paper flashing. For sliders with a nailing flange or an extruded exterior trim that sits on top of the finished wall, I run a heavy bead of silicone caulking behind the flange or trim before installing the frame (see the photo above). I try to keep that bead of caulking back from the exposed edge of the trim so that the silicone doesn't squeeze out when I press the door into place.

A Transit and Fishing Line Make Straight Sills

Once the unit is in the opening and is sitting at the pencil marks I made during the dry fit, I tack each side jamb in place with a screw or with a half-driven nail through the face of the jamb or the nail flange. The slider sills that are 8 ft. long or less stay pretty straight, and I can usually secure the sill in place without adding shims.

For sills longer than 8 ft., I stretch a string between the jambs to make sure the sill is perfectly straight. The fluorescent nylon string that is common on construction sites is really too heavy for this task, sort of like using a framer's pencil for finish carpentry. My favorite string for straightening sills is

20-lb. braided Dacron® fishing line, the strong, thin backing that I use on my fly reels (available at any fishing store). I stretch the line tight between the side jambs and insert shims from the outside between the sill and the drain pan until the sill is even with the line.

Fortunately, almost all sliding doors have adjustable wheels. But for those that don't, the sills have to be set absolutely level and straight. The same is true for multiple adjoining units that have to be set accurately to ensure that the mullions and casings line up horizontally. For these situations I level both ends of each sill with a transit to put all the adjoining units at precisely the same level. Once the ends of the adjoining sills are shimmed to the same level, I stretch my string and insert any shims needed to make each sill perfectly straight.

After the sill is set, I work on the side jambs, shimming out each one until it touches the level evenly top to bottom (see the left photo below). I secure the side jambs with more screws or half-driven nails and wait until the door panels are installed before I fasten the side jambs permanently. After the side jambs have been shimmed, I measure the diagonal distance of the frame corner to corner as a final test to make sure the frame is square.

On sliders wider than 8 ft., I also test for cross-legged jambs, which happens when the jambs are not in precisely the same plane. With cross-legged jambs, the sill and the head jamb aren't parallel, and the doors panels might bind in their channels and won't slide smoothly no matter how much wax or silicone I use. I test for this condition by stretching strings diagonally between the corners (see the right photo below). I move the top of one jamb and the bottom of the opposite jamb in or out until the strings just touch in the middle.

For sliding doors without adjustable wheels, the sills have to be absolutely level and straight.

Shims bring the jamb out to the level. After the sill is leveled and the jambs are plumbed top to bottom, shims are inserted behind the jamb until the jamb touches the level.

Checking for cross-legged jambs. Strings stretched from corner to corner will touch in the middle if the jambs are in precisely the same plane, which ensures the door slides smoothly.

Most Door Panels Go in Top First

If the slider didn't come preassembled, the next step is putting in the door panels. The stationary panel is almost always installed before the active or sliding panel, and all stationary-door panels go into the frame top first.

In most cases, the head jamb has a channel that the panel fits into. After the door panel is lifted into the channel, the bottom is placed over the track on the sill. The panel is then slid into position against the jamb. Most sliding-door units have an additional threshold strip that snaps into the sill between the stationary panel and the strike jamb to lock the panel in place. The active panel then is installed top first in its own channel (see the photo below), and the wheels are adjusted down to lift the door off the track.

Adjust the Wheels to Make the Slider Parallel to the Jamb

The next step is adjusting the wheels on the active door. Some wheels have adjustment screws that are accessed through the leading and trailing edges of the door, and other types have adjustment screws accessible through the exterior face of the door just above each wheel. Turning the adjustment screws raises or lowers the wheels, which in turn affects the alignment of the door panel in the frame (see the photo on the facing page).

I adjust the wheels until the active-door panel is parallel to the jamb. At the same time I make sure the door still slides smoothly. Before trying to turn the adjustment screws, I pick up the door a little to relieve some of the weight on the wheel,

Most panels go in top first. The door panels are installed after the frame is secure in its opening. Most door panels slip into a channel in the head jamb first; then the bottom edge is set down over the track on the sill.

which is especially helpful with some of the larger, heavier door panels. While adjusting the wheels, I also keep an eye on the alignment at the center, making sure the stile of the sliding-door panel is even and parallel with the fixed panel and that the muntin bars, if there are any, stay lined up.

When I'm satisfied with the way the panels are set, I drive home the screws in the side jambs, placing additional shims behind the strike location. To get the head jamb perfectly straight, I stretch my string and shim the head down to the string. I then secure it with screws or nails.

A Moisture Barrier Seals the Outside of the Slider

In many parts of the country, door installers run strips of felt paper under the nailing flanges on the side jambs to weatherproof sliding doors. Here in California, where stucco is the most-common siding material, the seal around the slider definitely has to be waterproof. So we use a system that is recommended by many manufacturers as well as by the National Fenestration Rating Council.[CM]

After the nailing flanges have been bedded in caulking against the sheathing, we run another bead of caulking on top of the nailing flanges, and a layer of Moistop is pressed into the caulk. The side jambs are flashed first with the Moistop extending at least 8 in. above the head jamb. I then apply a length of paper flashing across the head jamb, again pressing it into a bead of caulk on top of the nailing flange. The flashing on the head jamb should be long enough to overlap the flashing on the side jambs.

In areas exposed to extreme weather, such as places near the ocean, we follow the same steps to waterproof doors and windows except that we use self-healing, adhesive-backed waterproof membrane instead of paper flashing.

Tuning the sliding panel. A screw is turned to raise or lower the wheel, which brings the edge of the sliding panel parallel to the jamb.

Screens Should Slide as Smoothly as Main Panels

Putting in the screens is probably the most frustrating part of sliding-door installation. If manufacturers were graded by the quality of their screen doors, a lot of them would fail miserably. The worst screen doors have little plastic wheels without bearings. Often, these wheels cannot be adjusted and instead rely on a spring to counterbalance the door. When you try to slide the door, it acts like a rocking horse, dragging first on the sill, then on the head.

I always install screens top first into the screen channel in the head. While lifting the door against the head jamb, I raise the screen over the sill and set the bottom wheels down on top of the track. If the bottom wheels don't clear the track, I engage the top of the screen, then gently set the screen down next to the lower track. I then lift the screen from the bottom and push each wheel up with a stiff putty knife guiding it onto the track (see the left photo below). The difficulty of screen installation seems to increase in direct proportion to the amount of wind. So pick a calm day or get an extra pair of hands to help on windy days.

Most screens have wheels that adjust up or down by turning a screw in the leading or trailing edge of the door (see the right photo below). If the sill has been installed level and straight, it usually takes just a slight adjustment to get the leading edge of the screen parallel to the jamb. If there are wheels on top as well, I reduce their tension until the door slides smoothly.

The best sliding screens I've seen are on Marvin® doors (Marvin Window and Door,

P. O. Box 100, Warroad, Minn. 56763; 800-346-5128). Marvin screens are suspended from an upper track, and the spring-loaded wheels on the bottom just keep the bottom of the screen in line. I place the Marvin screen door first on the lower track, and I make sure the door slides easily on its lower wheels. Then I climb a ladder and slip the upper wheels into the upper track. All the adjustments are made on the upper wheels by turning a single cam-action screw.

By their nature, slider screens tend to be flimsy, so it's not uncommon to see them come from the factory slightly out of square. An out-of-square screen usually doesn't glide smoothly and is difficult to line up with the jamb. But in most cases these parallelogram screens can be squared by applying diagonal pressure on the screen frame. If the wheels on the screen are not adjustable, racking the

A putty knife puts screen wheels on track. If the screen panel rides on spring-loaded wheels, a stiff putty knife can be used to depress the wheel and guide it onto its track.

Screws adjust the screen wheels. Screws in the edges of the screen adjust the height of the spring-loaded wheel as well as the tension on the springs to keep the screen from binding.

screen is often the only way to make it line up with the jamb.

Screen doors on wood sliders have bumpers to keep them from damaging the jambs. But if the screen has just a single bottom bumper, the wheels have a tendency to bounce off the track when the bumper hits the jamb. I make sure that there are bumpers at both the bottom and the top of the screen door so that the back of the screen hits the jamb evenly. And with all sliding screens, a little silicone spray on the track helps keep those wheels gliding smoothly.

Installing the Locks and Hardware

Most sliders come from the factory prebored for their latch hardware, although a few come with the strikes installed. Installing strikes is one area in which reading the instructions and mocking up the hardware really helps. The strikes have to be located after the doors and latches are installed.

Some latches, especially those on screen doors, have a jaw or hook that engages the strike when the latch is closed. To locate the strike for this type of latch, I extend the latch mechanism and slide the door up to the jamb. I make a mark on the jamb in line with the bottom of the latch jaw (see the near right photo at right), which is the location of the proper position for the opposing jaw on the strike.

Other slider locks are internal, and the strike seats inside the latch. To line these up, I engage the strike in the latch and slide the door up against the jamb. A sharp point on the backside of the strike marks the jamb to locate the proper position for the strike (see the far right photo at right). Some strikes have to be mortised into the jamb for the door to close properly. But I always install the strike on the surface of the jamb first to figure out how deep I need to make the mortise. I try not to mortise the strike too deep or to close the gap between the slider and the jamb entirely. Adequate room has to

be allowed for the weatherstripping, and too much pressure can jam the lock.

Speaking of pressure, you're probably wondering what happened at that lady's house. I discovered that the sill was sitting on a foundation anchor bolt that I was able to trim off with my reciprocating-saw blade slid under the sill. I needed to draw the oak sill down, so I drilled through it in three spots, first counterboring for wood plugs. I used concrete screws to pull down the sill, an easy way to go if you can't remove the sill to install anchors. Three screws sucked that sill right down, and adjusting the doors was easy after that. The lady thought I was a genius.

Gary M. Katz is a carpenter in Reseda, California, and the author of The Doorhanger's Handbook *(The Taunton Press, 1998).*

Locating the screen strike. For most screens and many sliding doors, the strike is located by sliding the panel over and making a mark in line with the latch jaw.

A point locates this strike. If the jaw is located on the strike instead of the latch, the strike is engaged in the latch, and the panel is slid to the jamb. A point on the back of the strike marks its location.

Retrofitting a Threshold

■ GARY M. KATZ

I used to install the ordinary type of metal thresholds available at hardware stores. Every time it rained, I'd worry. I'd worry about water sweeping in as the door swung open, water trickling in around the sides of the door or water entering through the screw holes. I'd worry about water warping a hardwood floor or staining a Persian rug.

Now I use ordinary thresholds only in protected openings. Experience has taught me that three-piece water-return thresholds are the safest bet. I often use thresholds made by Pemko Manufacturing (P. O. Box 3780, Ventura, Calif. 93006; 800-283-9988). A water-return threshold (see the drawing on the facing page) consists of a threshold, a drain pan, and an interlocking sill cover. Although a water-return threshold is a little tough to install, the techniques I use make it simple enough, and the extra effort is worthwhile because it saves all of that worrying when it rains.

This example involves a door and frame already in place. While new prehung-door units typically come with serviceable thresholds, the techniques discussed here could be used to add water-return thresholds to new doors.

Start with the Sill Cover

Sill covers are lifesavers. They are essentially the flashing for the threshold and cover the rough edge of a concrete slab or the exposed grain of a wood floor. They are also the perfect cure for elevation problems that can be created when, for example, a tile floor is laid right up to an original oak threshold and oak sill. This problem was the case in the door opening featured here.

I start by deciding how the sill cover should be notched around the jamb and exterior trim. Usually the sill cover butts against the door jamb or the brick mold (see the drawing on the facing page). On this job, a screened-door jamb had been added, and the sill cover had to remain behind that jamb so that the screened door would shut (see photo 1 on p. 76).

First, I cut the sill cover off square at the longest dimension needed, in this case from brick mold to brick mold. To cut the sill cover, I use a small circular saw equipped with a metal-cutting blade. (For more on cutting aluminum, see the sidebar on p. 79). With the sill cover cut off square, I tip it into the opening and align it with the back of

Water-Return Threshold

The drain pan and sill cover of a water-return threshold both act as flashing, capturing any water that makes its way under the door and directing it back outside. An aluminum screened-door jamb that appears in the photos has been omitted from this drawing for clarity.

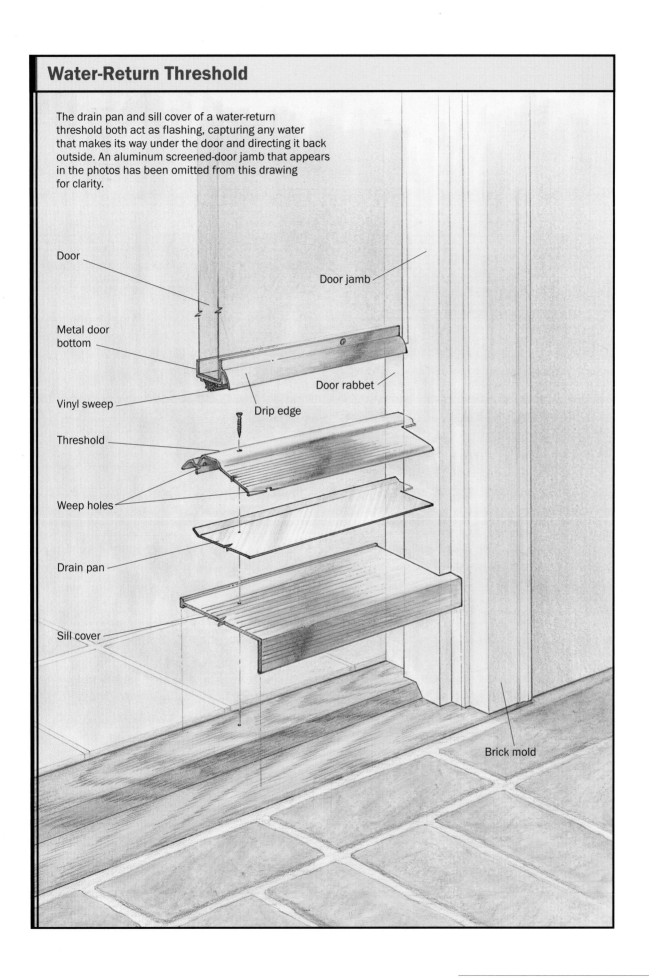

Door

Door jamb

Metal door bottom

Door rabbet

Vinyl sweep

Drip edge

Threshold

Weep holes

Drain pan

Sill cover

Brick mold

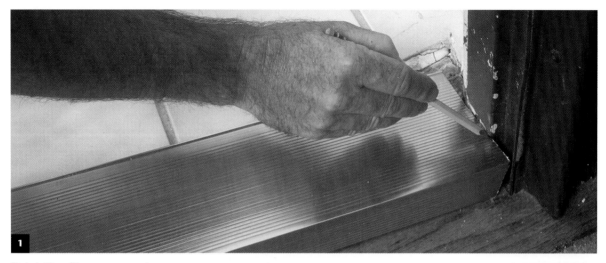

Notch the sill cover around the door frames. First, the broad, flat sill cover is held in place to mark the location and depth of the notch (1 and 2) that will allow the sill cover to fit around the jambs of the exterior door and the screened door.

the screened-door jamb and with the rabbet for the main door. Using a pencil or a utility knife (scratch marks made by a knife are easy to see on most aluminum products), I scribe marks for the notch (see photo 2). I repeat the process for the opposite side of the jamb. I'm using the jamb in place of a tape measure and square.

Slope the Sill Cover to Drain

After cutting the notches, I set the sill cover in place and prepare to trim the front, or vertical, edge of the cover. On some openings this step isn't necessary. But if there's a concrete porch or wooden step just beneath

the sill of the door, then the sill cover has to be scribed in. The cover must fit tight to the original sill, and it must have some slope so that water will drain outside, not inside.

I tip the sill cover and check the slope with a torpedo level; between ⅛ in. and 3⁄16 in. of pitch across the width of the sill cover is usually enough (see photo 3). Using anything handy, I shim the sill cover in place. Then, on the inside of the opening, I use my square to measure the distance between the sill cover and the floor beneath. I spread my scribes accordingly, and scribe a line across the front of the sill cover (see photo 4). Sometimes I attach a clean piece of masking tape to the sill cover to make the line easier to see. I put on my goggles and earplugs, and holding the sill cover as far

The sill cover slopes to the outside. The sill cover must be canted so that water can drain to the outside (3). Consequently, the front edge must be lowered by scribing it to the existing threshold, which is left in place (4). Masking tape makes the scribe line easier to see.

from my face as possible, I cut to the line with my circular saw.

Start with the Longest Dimension

I start fitting the threshold the same way I fit the sill cover, by measuring the widest dimension of the door opening, the rabbet for the main door. After making the first cut for overall length, I slide the threshold into the opening to mark the notch (see photo 5).

Normally, the threshold aligns with the face of the door, but for this opening I wanted to pull the threshold inside the house ¼ in. so that it would cover the raw edge of the tile. I tip the threshold, hold it against the jamb and mark the notches (see photo 6). I repeat these steps for the opposite end and cut the notches.

Once the threshold is cut, I temporarily set it in place on top of the sill cover. I mark the spot where the front edge of the threshold rests on the sill cover. This mark will determine the location of the drain pan, which is installed between the threshold and the

Scribe the threshold to the door frame. Rather than taking measurements and then transferring them to the threshold, the author holds the threshold itself against the jamb and carefully marks the locations of notches with either a pencil (5) or a knife (6).

Door height is transferred from the jamb to the door itself. Once the sill cover and threshold have been notched and set in place, the height at which the bottom of the door will be cut off can be determined (7). The mark made on the jamb takes into account the thickness of the metal-door bottom (8). The author then scribes the bottom of the door (9) to the new sill cover. Masking tape on the bottom of the door makes the pencil line easier to see.

sill cover. It's important to locate the drain pan carefully so that it catches water seeping through weep holes in the threshold but at the same time remains hidden from view.

I set the drain pan in position just behind the mark on the sill cover, then scribe a line for the notch I need to make around the jamb. The thin drain pan is easy to cut with tin snips.

With the drain pan cut and in place, I set the threshold on top of it and drill pilot holes for the screws that hold the assembly to the floor. If I'm working on a concrete slab, I run my masonry bit through the threshold, drain pan, and sill cover, down into the concrete. That's the surest method I know of getting concrete anchors in the right spots.

Cutting Off the Door

With the threshold and the sill cover in position, I'm ready to determine how much to cut off the bottom of the door. To get a weather-tight seal, this type of threshold requires a separate U-shaped metal door bottom with a vinyl sweep and drip edge (see the drawing on p. 75); in this case I used one made by Pemko Manufacturing. In some installations, there is enough room for the metal door bottom between the bottom of the door and the new threshold. In this case, though, the door is too close to the threshold and has to be trimmed slightly. First, I measure up from the top of the threshold ½ in. and make marks on both jamb legs (see photo 7). Then I remove the threshold and drain pan, but I leave the sill cover. The cover provides a smooth surface for me to run my scribes along.

I spread my scribes from the sill cover up to the line I've made on the jamb (see photo 8), then shut the door and scribe a line across the bottom of the door (see photo 9). Again, masking tape makes it easier to see the line.

I use different methods for cutting off doors. On veneered doors I sometimes use

A **site-built tool** speeds the cut. The author cuts doors with a "shooting stick," a plywood straightedge that has a fence against which he registers the table of his circular saw.

a "shooting stick" straightedge made of thin plywood (see photo 10). The shooting stick allows me to cut doors quickly without worrying about tearout. If I don't have my shooting stick with me, I use a metal straightedge and a knife to score a line on the door before I cut it. Either way, it's my circular saw that does the hard work.

Seal the Threshold with Plenty of Silicone

Before I install anything, I sweep out all of the dust and dirt, especially under the sill cover. I run a bead of silicone under the sill cover to help secure it, though the screws that pass through the threshold really do that job. I press the sill cover into the silicone and then run another bead of silicone on top of the sill cover and beneath the drain pan. I take care to keep the silicone away from the front edge of the drain pan so that it doesn't squeeze out. Then I press

Take Care When Cutting Aluminum

Cutting aluminum thresholds is not my idea of fun, so I like to do it as quickly and as safely as possible. Many people use hacksaws. Some professional weatherstrippers use portable tablesaws with aluminum-cutting blades.

I use a 4$\frac{3}{8}$-in. Makita® model 4200N trim saw (Makita U. S. A., 14930 Northam St., La Mirada, Calif. 90638; 800-462-5482) that cuts at a fast 11,000 rpm and a fine-toothed, combination metal blade, also by Makita (model 792334-2). I've used carbide-tipped blades to cut aluminum, but they are expensive, especially when the teeth begin to break off. (Makita no longer makes the 4200N, although some distributors still have a few of these saws. It was replaced with the model 5005 trim saw, which has a larger and slower-turning 5$\frac{1}{2}$-in. blade.)

Wearing eye protection is important when cutting aluminum, not only to guard against bits of flying metal but also because teeth on the combination blade can chip. In my work box I carry plastic goggles wrapped in a sock to prevent scratches. Years ago a bungee-cord accident took most of the vision in my left eye, so I'm careful with my right one. I also wear earplugs.

First the weatherstripping, then the door bottom. Weatherstripping is installed on the side jambs first. The drip cap on the door bottom then is scribed and notched to fit around the weatherstripping (11 and 12).

the drain pan down into the silicone and apply more silicone at the joint of the jamb and drain pan. I also squirt silicone into the screw holes. Finally, I set the threshold and screw it down snug.

It's better to notch the metal door bottom around the weatherstripping on the door jamb, so I install the weatherstripping first if there isn't any already. The door bottom has to be cut to fit the overall width of the door and then notched to fit around the weather-stripping on the door jambs (see photos 11 and 12).

Not Too Tight, Not Too Loose

After cutting the door bottom, I slip it on again and swing the door shut to make sure everything fits. The door bottom shouldn't be too long and squeeze or rub against the weatherstripping, but it should come close. I press the door bottom down against the threshold, but not too hard. The vinyl sweep needs to contact the threshold, but shouldn't be forced against it. Otherwise, the sweep will compress over time, and the seal will be lost.

I drive one screw at each end of the door bottom to hold it in place. Then I check the action of the door to be sure that it's sealing but that it's not rubbing too hard. Then I drive in the rest of the screws.

All that's left then is to apply silicone to the threshold and sill cover at the joint of the jamb, and maybe a little caulking between the door bottom and the door to seal out moisture. Before I leave, I check the swing of the door one more time. When it's right, the door closes just like a refrigerator, and with that whoosh of air, I'm gone.

Gary M. Katz is a carpenter in Reseda, California, and the author of The Doorhanger's Handbook *(The Taunton Press, 1998).*

Shopping for Interior Doors

■ CHARLES BICKFORD

We associate doors with choices. Remember the short story called "The Lady or the Tiger"? Or Monty Hall whipping the audience into a frenzy by asking, "What's behind door no. three?" The most intriguing thing about a door might be what it conceals. If you're building a house or an addition, though, you've got to pay attention to the door itself. What do you want from a door? Your front door keeps out the cold and other uninvited guests. Inside, doors perform a host of functions, from making a bathroom a more private place to isolating a noisy television to announcing the end of an argument. At a minimum, interior doors are large pieces of millwork and part of a room's overall design.

When buying a door, you'll want to know what the door is made of and how much it costs. Those of you on the lookout for a new door have to weigh the virtues of hollow vs. solid vs. stile and rail, flat panel or raised panel, veneered or solid panel, veneered and engineered composite panel or molded, and then a whole raft of wood species, among other things. To learn more about doors, I talked to manufacturers, visited their factories, talked to carpenters who install doors, and finally checked prices at door retailers

here in southern New England. I'll give you a preview of what you can expect at the door store.

Wooden Stile-and-Rail Doors Are Traditional and Sturdy

When someone says the word *door*, I think of a stile-and-rail door made of wood (see the bottom photo on p. 85). A wooden door sounds good when you rap on it with your knuckles. Its moldings and panels give the door visual depth and crisp symmetry. At $1\frac{3}{8}$ in. thick and about 60 lb., a typical interior door has the right amount of mass to swing easily on its hinges and to stop sound from traveling room to room. But according to studies commissioned by the National Wood Window and Door Association, I'm living in the past. Wooden stile-and-rail doors now account for less than 10 percent of the interior doors sold annually in the United States.

Still, the stile-and-rail door has been the door of choice for hundreds of years because its frame was more stable than its predecessor, the board-and-batten door. By loosely

When buying a door, you'll want to know what it is made of and how much it costs. You'll need to weigh matters such as hollow vs. solid vs. stile and rail, types of paneling, and types of wood.

capturing the panel (the widest and most unstable part of the door) in a rigid frame, the stile-and-rail door lets panels expand and contract seasonally without causing the door to stick or warp.

The advantages of a rigid frame still don't overcome the wood's natural tendency to move. The stiles and rails themselves must be made from flat, straight-grained stock that will resist meteorological temptations, and even then, doors still occasionally warp.

Although you can still buy doors made of solid wood, most wood doors are made of finger-jointed and veneered stock. This construction has two distinct advantages: One, the laminated frame won't warp as easily, and two, smaller pieces of lesser-quality wood are substituted for increasingly rare and expensive old-growth lumber.

I witnessed the process at a large door factory owned by Jeld-Wen® Inc. (P. O. Box 1329, Klamath Falls, OR 97601-0268;

The stile-and-rail door has been the door of choice for hundreds of years because its frame was more stable than its predecessor, the board-and-batten door.

800-535-3936), a facility that makes approximately 20,000 doors a week. Pine logs are sawn into usable lengths and widths; large knots and defects are discarded. Each piece is then sorted by size; smaller pieces are finger-jointed and glued into long runs of stile-and-rail stock, which are then veneered and shaped for assembly. The amount of waste at the end of the process is negligible; anything that can't be used for finger-jointing is shredded to make hardboard.

In addition to veneering frames, manufacturers apply the same thinking to panels. A stile-and-rail door can have two, three, four, five or six panels that can be raised or flat. In a door that's meant to be stained or clear finished, raised panels are traditionally made of solid wood; flat panels are cut from veneered plywood or composite. With a paint-grade door, doormakers usually won't use solid wood for the panels; when the wood moves (and it will move), an unpainted, unsightly line shows at the panel's perimeter. Medium-density fiberboard (MDF) panels are better: They can be shaped to any profile, they take paint beautifully, and best of all, they don't shrink or swell. Manufacturers are also now veneering MDF panels for stain-grade doors. If you are ordering custom paint-grade doors and think you must have solid-wood panels, have the shop prime and paint the panels before the door is assembled. When the panel shrinks, no unpainted line will show.

You can buy the most popular style, a six-panel door of standard size made of veneered Ponderosa pine, for just under $100*. The same door veneered in fir goes for about $200, while a door made of oak

might cost over $300. Some custom builders I've talked to spend the extra $10 to $15 for 1¾-in.-thick exterior doors and use them as bedroom doors; the additional ⅜ in. helps dampen sound and gives the door a more substantial feel.

French Doors Are Increasingly Popular

Single doors with lites are called sash doors; matched pairs are usually called French doors. The stile-and-rail construction, identical to that of paneled doors, gives the door frame its strength. To secure the glass, small pieces of trim called sticking are nailed or stapled to the muntins and bars. Morgan Door (Morgan Industries, 500 Park Plaza, Oshkosh, WI 54903-2246; 920-235-7170) has a newer method of installing glass called "compression glazing." Glass is captured in dadoes during the door's assembly, eliminating the applied sticking that typically holds the glass. What about a broken pane? Doug Tyriver of Morgan says that the percentage of breaks is negligible, but if a pane does get broken, the sticking can be routed out and replaced in the traditional manner.

More recently, manufacturers have begun to offer large single panels of glass that are divided with a V-groove etched into the glass (see the photos at left), which certainly makes finishing the door and cleaning the glass much easier. Like the other doors, sash doors are available in a dizzying assortment of divided lites, sash-and-panel arrangements, beveled glass, etched oval panels and leaded glass. Whatever the configuration, the doors must always have tempered glass. A pair of prehung French doors in pine can set you back about $500; add $100 to $150 if you want beveled glass; and double the price if you like the look of brass caming (trim) around the glass. Other species such as oak and fir are common options for stain-grade doors.

Etched grooves replace wood muntins and bars in sash doors. Some door manufacturers are now offering sash doors with large single lites divided by etched V-grooves, making the door easier to finish and to clean.

What's Inside a Door?

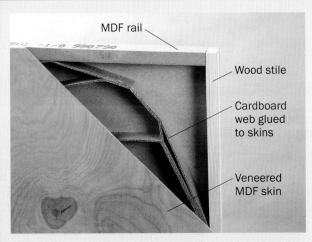

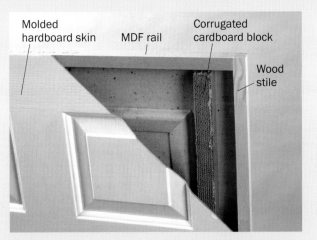

Flush-door construction. Flush doors are strong, light, and stable because the skins and frames reinforce each other. The door's interior is supported with a web of corrugated cardboard.

Molded hardboard's beauty is skin deep. Made from compressed wood fibers, these hardboard skins can be stamped into a variety of designs. Only ⅛ in. thick, the skins have a density similar to maple.

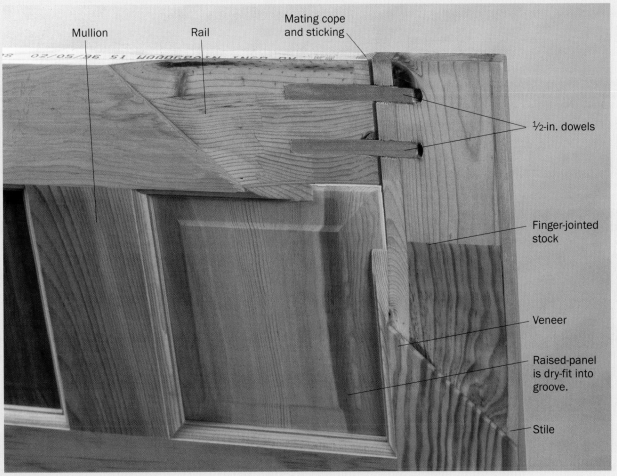

Stile-and-rail door construction. Modern stile-and-rail doors are built from finger-jointed and veneered lumber, which minimizes wood movement and maximizes lumber use. Doweled joints are strong and assemble quickly.

Louvered Doors Aren't Just for Decoration

Before the advent of air-conditioning, louvered doors were a necessity in hot, semitropical climates. They allowed air to circulate while keeping direct sunlight and prying eyes at bay. These ventilated doors are also used in colder regions to vent hot water-heater closets, furnace rooms, and damp basement closets.

You'll find most of these doors with louvers that are fixed in the open position. Better-quality doors feature louvers that are mortised into the stiles. Usually a custom item, movable louvers are handy for controlling the flow of air or sunlight into a space; cleaning the inevitable dust that collects between the slats is easier, too. Some door stiles even have nylon inserts that ease wood-on-wood friction.

A standard-size prehung louvered door costs about $140, either full louvered or a louver and lower solid-panel arrangement. As with exterior shutters, the best way to finish a louvered door is either to spray it or pay someone else to do the job.

Bifold doors also come in louvered styles, as well as flush, solid six panel or mirrored. Retailers are stocking more molded-skin bifolds as well (more about molded skin later). Bifold doors are somewhat limited in their individual sizes, from 9 in. to 24 in., but can be hung in groups of two or four to cover up to 8 ft. of doorway. A common problem with bifolds is that some doors warp more easily because they're made from thinner stock, a problem that can be compounded when the door is louvered. A 4-ft.-wide flush unit may cost under $100, whereas a mirrored set can fetch upward of $300. Café doors, those sawed-off louvered doors elbowed aside by movie cowboys, can be had with panels or with louvers, and each pair costs between $150 and $200 for a 30-in. opening.

> *A common problem with bifolds is that some doors warp more easily because they're made from thinner stock.*

Flush Doors Are Sometimes Hollow but Never Empty

The most inexpensive door on the market is the flush door, a simple flat rectangle that consists of a thin wooden frame covered on both sides by a ⅛-in. layer of plywood or hardboard called a skin (see the top left photo on p. 85). (The term *flush* refers to a detail of the manufacturing process. Oversize sheets of plywood or hardboard are glued onto frames; after the glue is dry, any excess is trimmed flush to the frame.) During the housing boom that followed World War II, these doors became popular because their materials were cheaper, and they were easy to manufacture, hence a lower retail cost. These days, flush doors and their molded-skin cousins account for approximately 90 percent of the residential interior-door market.

All flush doors have frames that consist of finger-jointed or solid-wood stiles and rails. Some manufacturers also substitute MDF for wood in the rails (and sometimes stiles) of their less expensive doors. A block of wood or MDF, known as the lock block, is glued on the strike side of the door and gives the installer a place to drill holes for the doorknob. (Flush doors commonly have a lock block on either side to make the door reversible.) The void in the middle of the door is filled according to the type of door. Hollow cores are filled with a corrugated cardboard web (see the photo on the facing page). *Hollow core*, sometimes used to describe any flush door, is a slight misnomer. They seem hollow because they weigh about 30 lb., half the weight of a solid stile-and-rail door, and don't have the mass to close as easily as a solid door. A favorite among eavesdroppers, hollow doors don't do much to stop kicking feet, either.

Paint-grade doors are usually clad in hardboard skins that have smooth textures or embossed grains and can be ordered

Hollow-core doors assemble in a snap. After gluing the stile, rails, and lock block to one hardboard skin, workers unfold corrugated cardboard onto the center of the door and lay the second skin down; the entire process takes less than ten seconds.

prestained in a variety of faux species. Birch, oak, and lauan are commonly used for plywood or MDF veneers; their cost and appearance depends on the type of veneer cut (rotary, plain sliced, bookmatched) and species. A plain lauan slab (a term used to describe doors before they receive hardware) may cost $20; a birch door with bookmatched veneers may go for up to $100.

Particleboard Gives Solid-Core Doors Their Heft

Solid-core flush doors are the Mack trucks of the door world. Filled with particleboard or MDF, these doors weigh about 80 lb. without their hinges. This extra weight gives the door a solid feel when it swings shut, a trait that rates high with your average consumer.

Doors filled with gypsum, normally used commercially for fire doors, weigh even more and are occasionally used in homes for extra fire protection. Another advantage of solid-core doors is their ability to dampen sound transmissions and to resist the antics of drunken frat boys.

The extra weight, however, puts a strain on hinges and jambs, especially on MDF jambs; replacing the middle hinge screw with a 3-in. screw can keep the smaller screws from pulling out of the jamb. You will also feel the strain if you have to hang these heavyweights all day. Solid-core doors are available in the standard array of hardboard plywood veneers and molded skins, and they cost about $30 more than their lightweight brethren.

Ordering Doors

Once you've picked a style that you like, there are other questions to consider before purchasing a door.

Door Size Is Measured in Feet and Inches

Doors come in a variety of standard sizes. The dimensions of a door are always referred to in feet and inches and are marked on the top rail of the door (see the top photo at right); an interior door that's 30 in. wide and 80 in. tall is marked as a 2-6, 6-8 door (spoken "two-six, six-eight"). You can order door heights from 6-0 to 7-0, but 6-8 is the industry standard for interior doors, although 8-0 (96 in.) doors are becoming a stock item in the West and Southwest. Doors are usually available in widths from 12 in. (for closets and bifolds) to 36 in., graduated in 2-in. increments. If you are replacing a door in an odd-size frame, be aware of how much door you can safely cut away. One of the problems with hollow flush doors is that there is a limited amount of door to trim before you hit air and ruin the door. Check the manufacturer's recommendations before you start to cut.

Prehung or Not?

If you are buying a houseful of doors, you might consider having the doors prehung. A prehung door has its hinges mortised into a solid jamb assembly and arrives at the job site ready to be shimmed and nailed into the opening (see the photo on the facing page). The casing is then nailed to the jamb.

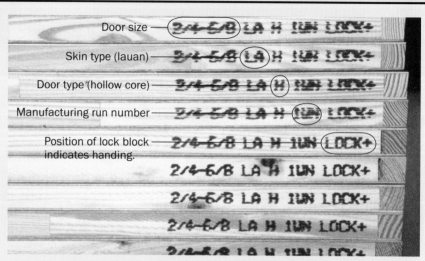

Door size	
Skin type (lauan)	
Door type (hollow core)	
Manufacturing run number	
Position of lock block indicates handing.	

To find out about the door, read the top rail. Manufacturers stamp pertinent information such as the door's size, the type of skin and core, handing, and the run number on the top rail.

Split-jamb doors are prehung and precased. The nesting arrangement of the two jamb halves, shown here from the bottom of the jamb leg, allows the jamb to span irregular wall thicknesses. Jambs are nailed through the door stop and casings.

An experienced door hanger can install a prehung unit in about 20 minutes, which more than makes up for the additional charge of prehanging, usually between $30 and $40 for pine jambs. For a little more money, you can customize the units by specifying types of jamb stock, hinges, and casing.

The split-jamb prehung door is a variation found in the Eastern United States and costs about the same as a solid jamb. This split jamb consists of two halves that join at the door stop, one side nesting into the other (see the bottom photo on the facing page). This arrangement allows the jamb's width to expand as much as $\frac{1}{2}$ in. to cover any deviations in the plane of the wall. Both jamb sides have the casing already attached. Once half of the jamb is centered and plumbed in the opening, the casing is nailed to the wall, and the remaining half can be slid into place and nailed. Although you might see split jambs outfitted with inexpensive clam-shell or colonial casing, you can often get other stock moldings for a few more dollars.

The Western cousin to the split jamb is called a prefit jamb. The head and legs of the jamb arrive at the job site unassembled, but each piece has casing nailed to both sides. The casing on each piece cups over the drywall, the head and legs interlock, and the casing is nailed off. Some prefits also feature a screw at the top of each leg that bears on the trimmer stud and can be tightened or loosened to center the door in the opening.

Keep in mind that although a prehung door comes with hinges and is bored for a passage set, it won't come with the passage set unless you specify it. Sometimes a millwork distributor will offer free passage sets, but usually these sets are cheap and not worth your attention.

Handing a Door

One of the more confusing aspects of doors is the issue of "handing": What makes a left-hand door left

Prehung doors ready for a carpenter. Doors hinged into preassembled frames await shipping to the job site. An experienced door hanger can install and trim a prehung unit in about 20 minutes.

and a right-hand door right? Ask five carpenters, and you'll get at least five different answers. Scott Whitten, a veteran door salesman at House of Doors in Cheshire, Connecticut, tells his customers to face the door. If the door opens toward you with the knob on the left, it's a left-hand door; if the knob is on the right, it's a right-hand door. This method works for French doors as well; the active door determines the handing of the set. The handing is normally marked at the top of the door's rail and/or on the back of a prehung jamb.

Warranties

All large door manufacturers offer a warranty with their product. Nearly all say the owner must seal all six sides of the door for the warranty to be in effect. The warranty also covers warping or twisting in excess of $\frac{1}{4}$-in. deflection over the total length of the door but may not cover warpage on doors over 36 in. wide and 84 in. long.

Molded Doors Are Flush Doors with a New Suit of Clothes

Developed in the early 1970s by companies such as Weyerhaeuser®, Masonite®, and Caradco®, molded-skin doors (see the top right photo on p. 85) now account for roughly half of the flush-door market, or about 15 million doors a year. The doors share the same internal construction as their flat cousins but are covered with hardboard skins molded in the shape of traditional stile-and-rail doors.

Manufacturers such as Masonite and Jeld-Wen process wood scraps, sawdust, and other wood detritus into a soft, fuzzy mass of clean wood fibers that is mixed with binders and loosely pressed into long mats that resemble sheets of damp oatmeal. The mats are then fed into enormous stamping presses that heat and compress the sheets into ⅛-in. door skins. These skins are stamped with a wide variety of designs that include smooth or wood-grained surfaces, arched or straight rails, and different panel configurations.

As with other types of hollow doors, the molded door frames are lightweight (stile-and-rail members are 1⅛ in. sq.); the strength of the door lies in the lamination of frame and skin. Molded doors are also available with solid cores. Masonite (Masonite Corp., 1 Wacker Drive, Suite 3600, Chicago, IL 60606; 800-405-2233) also makes a solid door it calls Craft-Core; the company claims the door, filled with a composite lighter than the standard particleboard, weighs as much as a solid-wood door but has the dimensional stability of MDF.

Molded doors tend to be as stable as other flush doors. The skins resist abuse fairly well, too, having a density similar to hard maple. The weakest of the bunch, according to several tradesmen I talked to, are doors with MDF stiles. Larry Hart, a veteran door hanger from southern California, told me that he won't install MDF-edged doors in bathrooms because the composite tends to wick moisture and warp the doors.

Molded-skin doors have been growing in popularity in the past ten years, mainly due to their low cost (starting at about $40), low maintenance, and resemblance to more expensive stile-and-rail doors. The skins can be painted or stained, although the latter finish can be tricky to execute properly. For an additional $15 to $25, you can order prefinished molded doors as well.

Look for Newer Door Materials in the Future

As in other areas of the building trade, there is a strong trend in the door industry toward manufactured materials such as hardboard and other composites that are both dependable and inexpensive. Other materials that are sure to appear on the market include fiberglass, rigid-foam cores, and carbon-fiber laminates. As long as the door looks good, closes evenly, withstands years of abuse and slams good and loud when you want it to, it shouldn't matter what materials are used in the door—we can always use the wood somewhere else.

*Note prices are from 1998.

Charles Bickford is a senior editor at Fine Homebuilding.

Disappearing Doors

■ GARY M. KATZ

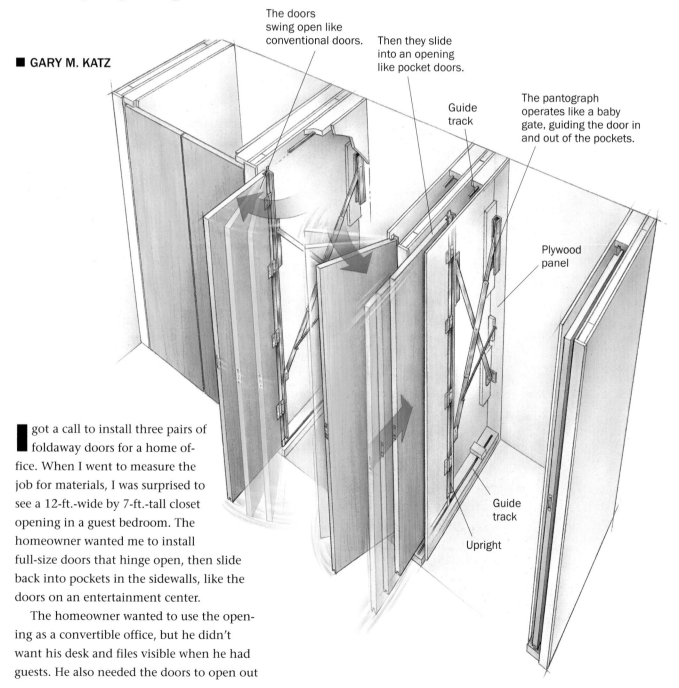

The doors swing open like conventional doors.

Then they slide into an opening like pocket doors.

Guide track

The pantograph operates like a baby gate, guiding the door in and out of the pockets.

Plywood panel

Guide track

Upright

I got a call to install three pairs of foldaway doors for a home office. When I went to measure the job for materials, I was surprised to see a 12-ft.-wide by 7-ft.-tall closet opening in a guest bedroom. The homeowner wanted me to install full-size doors that hinge open, then slide back into pockets in the sidewalls, like the doors on an entertainment center.

The homeowner wanted to use the opening as a convertible office, but he didn't want his desk and files visible when he had guests. He also needed the doors to open out

This system is ideal for hiding a home office, a walk-in closet, a laundry room or a display case because the doors can be kept out of the way when open.

Sources

The Hawa-Turnaway hardware is available from:

Häfele®
800-423-3531
$546 per door, plus shipping and handling.
www.hafeleonline.com

of the way so that he wouldn't feel as if he were working in a closet, and he had just the hardware for the job.

To familiarize myself with the Hawa-Turnaway hardware, I opened one box. Like most carpenters, I set aside the instructions until I could understand the function of the hardware. After fooling with the two colossal aluminum pantographs, what I called the scissors, I began to understand the operation. The pantograph ensures that the doors glide in and out of the sidewall pocket.

But I knew I was in trouble once I opened the directions: "Warning! This product must be installed to exact dimensions in a precision-built cabinet. Do not attempt to install this product in a rough opening on a job site." I showed this warning to the general contractor and the homeowner, and they asked me to take the job and to do my best.

The key to installing the system properly is getting the top and bottom tracks level, plumb and perfectly parallel; otherwise, the doors bind in the track and do not open or close properly (see the drawing on p. 91).

I installed the upper and lower plastic U-shaped tracks in wood blocks because the doors needed to clear a carpeted floor and a head jamb. Creating a perfectly level plane was a prerequisite for this job. The floor was miserably out of level (see

photo 1 on the facing page), but I could shim the blocks pretty easily (see photo 2). In addition, the blocks acted as backing cleats for the plywood panels needed to create the pocket walls. I used a plunge router to cut the dadoes in the blocks for the tracks, then installed and shimmed them level. Installing the top blocks was much easier (see photo 3).

The back of the large pantograph was mounted to the sidewall in two locations: I bolted the top to the wall, but the bottom had to be mounted in a vertical track secured with Allen-screw pins so that the pantograph could be adjusted (see photo 4). I fastened the doors to leaf hinges that mounted in a track on the front of the pantograph. By sliding the hinges in the track, I could raise and lower each door, so aligning the tops of all the doors was a snap. Adjustable steel guides keep the hardware on track.

I wouldn't recommend that just anyone take on a pair of full-size foldaway doors—not to mention three of them. But with some careful planning and patience, installing this precision hardware can result in a smoothly operating, slick pair of hidden doors (see photo 5).

Gary M. Katz is a carpenter in Reseda, California, and the author of The Doorhanger's Handbook *(The Taunton Press, 1998).*

If the Frame Isn't Perfect, the Doors Won't Work

1. **Leveling the bottom tracks** is the single most important step. A long level establishes the high point of the floor. Level lines are marked where the 2x4 blocks need to lie.

2. **Fixing the dips.** After the opening is leveled, the 2x4 blocks are shimmed to create a level floor plane.

3. **Keeping it in line.** The top rails are installed by measuring up from the leveled bottom blocks, are checked for level, and are held plumb to the bottom rail.

4. **Final adjustments** are no big deal. The arm of the pantograph is adjusted so that it will not overextend the pocket and so that the door slips back flush to the opening.

5. **Custom doors finish the job.** Although the author chose light, hollow-core doors, the hardware can handle an 80-lb. door.

Get the Right Replacement Window

DANIEL S. MORRISON

Almost 58 million windows are sold every year, and more than half of them are replacement windows. About 30 percent of the windows being replaced are less than 10 years old, and many are only 2 years old. Why are so many new windows being replaced? Many fail due to bad installation, but most windows being replaced simply haven't lived up to homeowners' expectations for comfort or durability. Getting a window that matches your needs and expectations involves a series of decisions and trade-offs. But among the many variables—such as materials, features, and warranties—good installation is essential. A poor installation practically will guarantee failure of even the most expensive high-performance window.

There's more than one way to replace your windows, and the most appropriate system depends on why you're replacing them in the first place. If the old windows are rotted out or show signs of water damage, it's critical to address the cause of the water damage in the replacement. If your old windows are merely cloudy, drafty, or hard to operate, the options widen.

Begin by Choosing a Type

The simplest, most common replacement-window systems leave intact the existing window frame along with the interior and exterior trim. When water damage isn't a problem, these systems offer excellent options, including sash replacement and complete window inserts.

Water-damaged windows indicate a leak and should be removed and replaced with new window units (Option 3, p. 100). This scenario entails removing the interior and exterior trim and possibly the siding and drywall. Fixing the leak and properly flashing, air-sealing, and waterproofing the new window are critical to avoid repeating the initial water damage.

Some companies even offer energy-efficient historic reproductions that closely match original windows (see "Historic Houses Don't Need Leaky Windows," p. 99).

Frame and Sash Choices: Think Aesthetics, Insulation, Durability

Whichever option you choose, you have to decide what materials best fit your needs. If you like wood windows but don't like scraping and painting every 10 years, exterior

Quick Guide to Choosing

FIRST ASK, "WHY REPLACE?"
- **Water damage:** The windows need surgery. See Option 3, p. 100.
- **Early failure:** If no water damage, Option 1 or 2 will do; see p. 96 or p. 98.
- **Comfort/energy-performance upgrade:** Option 1 or 2 will do; see performance expectations below.
- **Hate to paint:** Option 1 or 2 will do; see maintenance expectations below.

NEXT ASK, "WHAT ARE MY PRIORITIES?"

Maintenance Expectations
(See "Sash and Frame Options," p. 100.)
- **Vinyl or fiberglass** (either clad or extruded) is best for coastal exposure.
- **Aluminum-clad** is durable but expensive.
- **Wood windows** can be durable and are less expensive.

Performance Expectations
(Energy efficiency, comfort, structural)
- **Good:** An EnergyStar sticker guarantees minimum EPA energy-efficiency standards (NFRC-certified).
- **Better:** Shop for better NFRC ratings based on your climate (see "Energy-Performance Ratings," p. 96).
- **Best:** Use the Web to model windows for specific (north, south) walls in your house (see "Sources," p. 101).

Durability Expectations
- **20+ years:** A solid warranty is most important. Other expectations will give way, particularly budget expectations.
- **10 years or less:** Comfort, maintenance, or aesthetics may trump warranty.

Option 1 (the Cheapest): Replace Only the Sash

If the existing frame and sill are in good condition, you can swap the sash for an energy-efficient upgrade. Remove the sash and parting stops, then install jamb liners against the sides of the window frame. The liners form a tight seal with the new sash. Many manufacturers have replacement-sash kits designed for their older frames.

COST: $260*
National average list price based on a 3-ft. by 5-ft. opening; aluminum-clad sash; low-e, low-SHGC, argon-filled, double-hung replacement window.

Energy-Performance Ratings: Lower Is Better

Because two windows that look exactly alike can perform differently, the National Fenestration Rating Council provides third-party performance ratings for windows and doors so that consumers can have an apples-to-apples comparison.
The invisible parts of a window combine to boost performance, energy efficiency, and comfort.

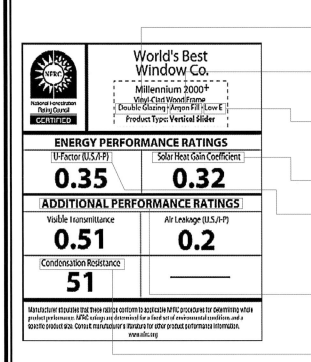

Double-glazing improves U-factor: Two layers of glass are standard. Triple-glazing is a good idea in very cold climates. Impact-resistant storm glazing is required in many coastal areas.

Gas filling: Like air, argon is nontoxic, clear, and odorless, but it's a better insulator. The optimal gap between panes of glass is ½ in.

Low-emittance (low-e) coatings are nearly transparent metal films. All low-e coatings bounce radiant heat back to you in the winter. Most reflect the sun's radiant heat in summer, too.

Solar heat-gain coefficient (SHGC): Percentage of the sun's radiant heat getting into your house. Low numbers (0.4) mean low AC bills. Medium and high numbers (0.5–0.7+) can work in colder climates.

U-factor is the inverse of R-value: Sum of all U-factors (glass, frame, and sash) in the window unit. Smaller numbers (0.35 or less) mean greater energy efficiency and comfort.

Warm-edge spacers: Specialized rubbers, foams, and plastics that improve U-factor and reduce condensation.

Additional performance ratings such as air leakage, water leakage, and impact performance may be required by local codes.

Condensation resistance: Quantifies all of the above features to predict the likelihood of condensation. This 0–100 index is intended more for comparing different windows than as a performance guide.

IMPORTANT INSTALLATION DETAILS

- Measure according to manufacturer's specifications.
- Check that window frame is square.
- Check that sill is flat, not crowned.
- Jamb liners and sash must match slope of sill precisely; kinks allow air leakage.
- Finish air-sealing with foam plugs at top and bottom of jamb liners.

PROS

- Easy installation.
- Energy-efficient upgrade.
- Maintains the window's original glass area.
- No need to disturb existing casings.
- Least-expensive replacement-window system.

CONS

- The finished product may be leakier than Options 2 and 3.
- Hard to fit properly in old openings that may be out of square or crowned.

Comfort Costs Less

I was sitting on the couch in the little window bay of my living room watching Norm on PBS℠ like I do every Saturday. It was springtime at *The New Yankee Workshop®*, but outside my windows, it was -10°F, and I was cold. I could have put on a sweater, as my wife does, but I did what most guys do: I reached for the thermostat. I was astonished to see that it read 70°F. How could that be? Since 70°F is warm, why was I uncomfortable?

Because heat loss from radiation is much more drastic than other types of heat loss, it gets worse as you get closer to the cold (or hot) object. Old or cheaply made windows can suck the heat from you in winter or turn your living room into a microwave in summer. Effectively, this makes the comfortable portion of a room smaller because you're uncomfortable if you sit near the windows. And if you're uncomfortable, you reach for the thermostat.

Good windows enlarge a room's comfortable area, which means less reaching for the thermostat, less work for your furnace or air-conditioner, and lower utility bills.

Option 2 (the Easiest): Insert a Frame and Sash

The most common system comes as a complete unit that slips into the existing window jambs against the exterior (or interior) window stops. Use low-expanding foam to seal the perimeter gap and ensure an airtight installation.

COST: $530*
National average list price based on a 3-ft. by 5-ft. opening; aluminum-clad sash; low-e, low-SHGC, argon-filled, double-hung replacement window.

cladding of vinyl, fiberglass, or aluminum is an excellent choice (see the photos in "Sash and Frame Options," p. 100). They're all durable and require no painting. Window manufacturers offer aluminum cladding in up to 50 stock colors with custom-color matching, whereas vinyl and fiberglass cladding are generally available in white and beige; fiberglass can be painted. Keep in mind that you can step down in price by choosing all-vinyl windows. They can be up to 40 percent less expensive than comparable aluminum-clad wood windows.

Because the frame and sash can make up almost a third of a window's total area, their materials play an important part in both comfort and durability. Insulating capacity (measured as U-factor; lower is better) is important in cold climates; in hot climates, keeping heat out of the house takes precedence. Because radiant heat is much more powerful than other forms of heat transfer, it's more important to keep radiant heat out with low solar-heat-gain coatings than to focus on U-factor.

Finally, consider how the frame and sash materials will stand the test of time. Some very good windows are made with vinyl,

and some very bad windows are made with vinyl. The same goes for wood and aluminum. Your durability decision shouldn't be based solely on material; quality of manufacture is equally important.

Look for Ratings, and Buy for the Warranty

It's important to realize that when you remove a window from a wall, you're left with a large hole in your house. You should plug that hole with something that will look good, perform well, and last long.

To increase the odds of meeting your comfort and durability expectations, you need to read the National Fenestration Rating Council's (NFRC's) energy-performance label and shop for the best warranty. "You can't trust your eyes when you're shopping for windows," says R. Christopher Mathis, a building consultant and former NFRC director. "Two windows that look exactly alike can perform very differently." Different glass coatings, gas fillings, and spacers between glass panels are impossible to differentiate visually; they can be verified only through laboratory tests. If you want the assurance of

IMPORTANT INSTALLATION DETAILS

- Verify opening for square; measure accordingly.
- Air-seal the perimeter with low-expanding foam, not fiberglass batts.
- Fill header and sill extensions with low-expanding foam insulation.
- Protect against wind-driven rain with highest-quality sealant at exterior stops.

PROS

- More dependable energy ratings than Option 1 because the sash and frame are tested as a unit.
- Less invasive than whole-window replacement. The process takes one hour.
- Won't disturb existing casings, siding, or wall coverings.

CONS

- Reduced glass area and bulkier look due to an additional window frame.
- Smaller opening may violate fire-code egress requirements.
- The most expensive method, considering only materials.

energy efficiency from an independent third party, you need to look for the NFRC label.

NFRC ratings make comfort expectations predictable; a solid warranty makes a window's service life predictable. Warranties reflect how confident a company is in the durability of its product. The top window companies offer 20/10 warranties: 20 years on the window seal and 10 years on everything else (frame, sash, and hardware). That's a good benchmark.

Prorated warranties and exclusions such as nontransferability make it hard to judge how long even NFRC-rated windows will perform well.

And beware of a lifetime warranty. If name brands such as Andersen, Marvin, and Loewen can give you only a 20/10 warranty, how can a no-name window company offer more? The answer: exclusions.

Can Mom and Pop Compete with Marvin and Pella®?

There are thousands of window manufacturers in North America. Smaller companies can produce a less-expensive product that

Historic Houses Don't Need Leaky Windows

Many window manufacturers offer historic retrofits (as illustrated here by Marvin) that will be more likely to pass the historic commission's review panel. Andersen®'s Woodwright series of replacement windows features wood jamb liners and traditional sash details to blend gracefully into a historic house. For more information on preservation guidelines, visit the National Park Service website at www2.cr.nps.gov.

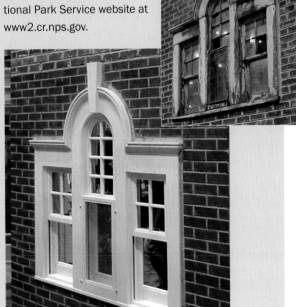

Option 3 (the Best): Complete Window Replacement

When water damage is occurring, the window and rotten framing should be replaced and the source of the leak tracked down and stopped. A rotted window may be the symptom, not the source, of the leak. Complete replacement is best because it allows you to integrate the new window fully into the wall with new head and pan flashings, low-expanding foam, flexible flashing membranes, and high-quality sealants.

COST: $446*

National average list price based on a 3-ft. by 5-ft. opening; aluminum-clad sash; low-e, low-SHGC, argon-filled, double-hung window.

IMPORTANT INSTALLATION DETAILS

- Protect against wind-driven rain with head flashing and high-quality sealant along top and side flanges; uncaulked bottom flange allows water to escape.

- Ensure against rot with pan flashing.

Sash and Frame Options: Choices Depend on Color, Cost, and Durability

VINYL WON'T CORRODE

Clad or extruded, vinyl is a no-maintenance option for coastal areas where aluminum may corrode over time.

U-factor: 0.33; with insulated cavity: 0.27

Colors: Whites, beiges

Relative cost: Least-expensive option; roughly 40 percent less than aluminum-clad.

WOOD REQUIRES A FINISH

Wood windows are available factory-primed, but you should scuff and reprime the surfaces before painting. With regular maintenance and good paint, wood windows ought to last a long time.

U-factor: 0.33

Colors: Any paint or stain color.

Relative cost: More expensive than vinyl.

FIBERGLASS IS THE MOST DURABLE

Stronger than vinyl, fiberglass can be extruded into slimmer cross-sectional profiles, making it a good choice for Option 2. Also available with wood interiors for a warmer look. No maintenance required, but fiberglass can be painted.

U-factor: 0.33; with air cavity filled: 0.27

Colors: White; can be painted.

Relative cost: Costs more than wood or vinyl.

- Integrate flashings shingle style into building paper.
- Maintain air seal with low-expanding foam along inside perimeter.

PROS

- Most versatile because you can change the window's size.
- The most energy-efficient system because the window is fully integrated into the wall.
- Most durable because you can upgrade the flashing details.

CONS

- The most invasive method.
- The most difficult method.
- The most expensive method, considering labor.

Sources

Energy-Efficient Window Information

www.efficientwindows.org

http://windows.lbl.gov

www.eere.energy.gov/consumer
info/energy_savers/windows.html

www.rehabadvisor.com

www.nfrc.org

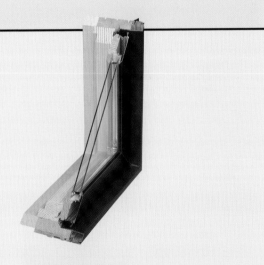

ALUMINUM-CLAD
COMES IN MANY COLORS

If you want to change the color, repaint with a metal bonding enamel after proper surface preparation.

U-factor: 0.33

Colors: Some companies have up to 50 colors; many will custom-match colors.

Relative cost: Most expensive option.

rivals the windows made by the big guys, but they usually can't provide the same warranty. Small companies have fewer risk-management resources, so some risk is passed to the consumer.

When shopping for the warranty, make sure that the window manufacturer will be there when you need it. Ask how long the manufacturer has been in business. Is a 2-year-old manufacturer offering you a 20-year warranty? Does the company have a toll-free number, and if so, is there an actual human being to answer your call?

You may decide that a prorated warranty is worth the gamble for the lower price, but stay away from nontransferability clauses; they don't make sense. How can the transfer of homeownership affect the service life of a building component?

Replacement windows are a big investment in money, energy efficiency, and personal comfort. Don't skimp on untested or falsely warrantied windows. If the company won't bet on its product, why should you?

*Note prices are from 2004.

Daniel S. Morrison *is an assistant editor at* Fine Homebuilding.

Restoring Window Sashes

■ DAVID GIBNEY

Other than a lighted match, nothing will ruin the charm of an old house faster than ripping out the original double-hung windows. But if your windows are old enough to have sash cords, pulleys, and weights—and especially if they've fallen into disrepair—you might be tempted by those ads that promise huge energy savings and no maintenance if you replace the windows. What they won't tell you is that energy-wise, you'd get a much better return on your investment simply by repairing existing windows and adding high-quality storm windows (see the sidebar on p. 105).

From my perspective, it makes no sense to remove window units that have survived for a century or more and to replace them with something that may not last a decade before the finger-jointed wood frame rots or the vinyl cladding deteriorates or the double-glazed seals rupture. Why not spend a little time, and a lot less money, to help your existing windows last another century?

They Don't Make Them Like They Used To

Materials vary by region, but most of the old windows that I see are crafted from first-growth, vertical-grain pine. This remarkable stuff is dimensionally stable and highly rot-resistant, far superior to anything available today. Old-growth pine is so durable and forgiving that even though they may look bad, most of the windows I'm asked to repair (or replace) generally require little more than minor touch-ups and a bit of reglazing.

If your house is 100 or more years old and if you're lucky, you still might have the original handblown glass. This important feature denotes early windows. Depending on when they were made and what raw materials were used, some window panes are rippled like the ocean, and others are bubbled or scattered with bull's-eyes. Each pane, though, is unique. On the rare occasion

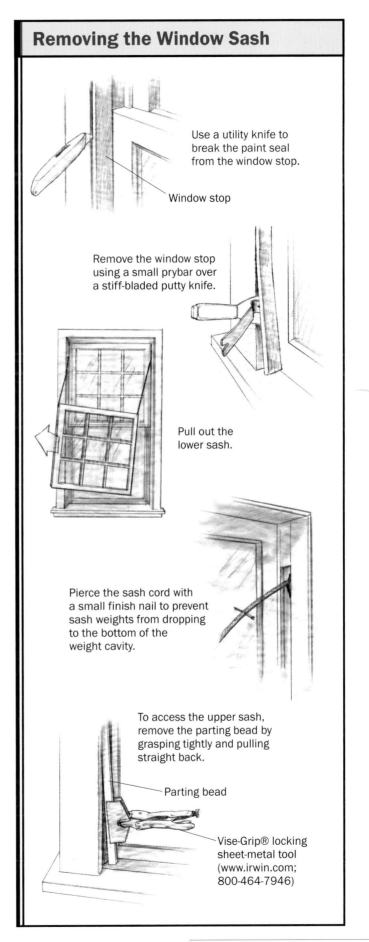

Removing the Window Sash

Use a utility knife to break the paint seal from the window stop.

Window stop

Remove the window stop using a small prybar over a stiff-bladed putty knife.

Pull out the lower sash.

Pierce the sash cord with a small finish nail to prevent sash weights from dropping to the bottom of the weight cavity.

To access the upper sash, remove the parting bead by grasping tightly and pulling straight back.

Parting bead

Vise-Grip® locking sheet-metal tool (www.irwin.com; 800-464-7946)

Removing Putty and Paint Is the Hard Part

If a window sash needs major repairs, both glass and paint usually have to come off. To get at the glass, I start by hand-scraping the outside of the frame where the wood meets the glazing putty; removing the overlapping paint helps break the bond between the two materials.

1. For putty removal, I depend mostly on a Fein MultiMaster (800-441-9878; www.feinus.com), which is set up with a vibrating scraper. Coming in flat over the glass loosens most of the putty, but it can be slow going. If the putty is rock hard, I attack first with my 3⅜-in. cordless Makita circular saw, but this process requires a skilled hand. I set the depth of the blade so that it will not touch the glass, then carefully cut alongside the shoulder of the frame. After the saw cut, the remaining putty goes quietly.

2. Once all the putty is gone, I slide a scraper along the surface of the glass to remove the old glazier's points.

3. To cut out any putty embedded between glass and wood, I run a knife blade along the edge of the glass. Then all it takes is a gentle push up from the bottom side to free the glass.

4. I use an electric paint remover (Warner Tool Products; www.warnertool.com; 877-992-7637) to strip the flat sections of the sash.

5. A heat gun in combination with a contoured scraper takes care of the profiles.

when I find a window that's not salvageable, I always save the glass.

If you're seeking sources for old glass, check first with salvage contractors in your area or with window-replacement contractors, most of whom will be happy to let you haul away the old sashes that they take out. If those options don't pan out, I know of one supplier (Fairview Glass Co.; www.fairviewglass.com; 301-371-3364) that ships glass nationwide.

Window Frames Rarely Need Fixing

I inspect the window frames as well as the sashes. Like a dentist with a pick, I use a scratch awl to poke around rotted areas to determine the extent of damage. Fortunately, unless the house in question has suffered from serious moisture problems, the frames are almost always rock solid, which is why so many manufacturers have come out with replacement window units that fit within existing frames. If I find some frame rot, it's usually confined to the end grain where the

side jamb meets the sill or to the top portion of the sill itself. These infestations are cleaned out and repaired easily with epoxy.

If serious damage has occurred, it's most likely to involve the sashes, particularly the lower sash, because they are used and abused the most. If sash rot is minor and localized, I make the repairs in place. But whenever I discover a serious problem such as a severely rotted bottom rail or side jamb, or a broken or rotted muntin strip, I remove that particular sash and make the repair in the shop. Only if the bottom and both sides are missing do I consider a sash to be beyond repair.

Disassembly Requires Care, Especially with Old Glass

As I remove each sash, I hold it up to a light source and take note of which panes of glass are original so that I remember to take special care to save them. Removing old glass without breaking it is a tedious process at

---

Storm Windows and Weatherstripping Tighten Up Old Windows

By today's standards, old double-hungs are drafty; but that problem is easy to fix. The most straightforward solution is to add storm windows. Triple-track units are the most common option, but they can be bulky and conspicuous. If you decide to go this route, buy from a high-end manufacturer that offers custom sizing and a wide choice of colors.

For a less conspicuous appearance, I prefer the Historic One-Light (HOL) unit from Allied Window Inc. (800-445-5411; www.alliedwindow.com). This low-profile storm (shown here) is essentially a single-track unit in which upper and lower sashes mount one over the other; screens are available, but they must be stored elsewhere.

For restoration purists who'd rather not see any storm window on the outside of a home, this manufacturer also offers a variety of interior storm-window options.

The windows themselves also can be tightened up. The edges of fixed sashes should be caulked, inside and out, to eliminate air infiltration. If you're willing to remove them from their frames, sashes and stops can be routed and retrofitted with specially designed weatherstripping. Resource Conservation Technology Inc. (410-366-1146; www.conservationtechnology.com) offers a wide variety of weatherstripping as well as an excellent catalog that doubles as an installation manual.

best. Sometimes I find that the old glazing putty is so loose that it just needs a good nudge with a paint scraper to get it off; oftentimes, however, the putty is as hard as rock.

Plenty of tools and techniques are available for removing stubborn old glazing putty, and none of them is perfect. I've had lots of success using a Fein MultiMaster tool along with a small Makita cordless circular saw to break up old putty, but this process is not for the squeamish (see the sidebar on p. 104).

If you've tried to remove the glass without success, you might be able to find a local window-repair or paint-removal specialist who can help. Or you might attempt the repair with the glass in place. You also might want to check out a new infrared paint-removal tool that claims to be equally effective for removing glazing putty.

Epoxy Repairs Minor Damage

After all the glass has been removed and carefully set aside, the built-up layers of paint are next to go. Old windows almost always have at least one layer of lead paint on them, so it's important to take some safety precautions. If I have an entire house's worth of windows to repair, I send them to a reputable paint stripper, where the paint can be removed safely. If I have just a few windows to repair, I strip the paint myself using low-temperature heat strippers (see

Repair Sash with Old Wood and Epoxy

1. Deep gouges and rot are carved out and squared up with a chisel to make room for a wooden patch (a dutchman) that's fastened with epoxy adhesive.
2. After all surfaces are wetted with epoxy, a thickener is added to the mix; a generous helping is applied between the dutchman and the sash.

3. Cut from the same wood species as the sash, the dutchman should stand slightly proud of the surrounding surfaces. After the epoxy has cured, the patch can be planed and sanded to make the repair invisible.

photo 5 on p. 104) or chemicals (Back to Nature Products; 800-423-7733; www.ibacktonature.com).

If the sashes have any minor cases of rot or simple weather damage, they are repaired with epoxy. First, I gently wire-brush the surface free of all loose wood fibers. Next, I carefully warm the wood surface with a heat gun set on its lowest setting. Using a disposable paintbrush, I apply generous amounts of a liquid epoxy (West System; 989-684-7286; www.westsystem.com); the heat treatment allows the liquid epoxy to travel deep into the wood's fibers, creating a superior bond. As soon as the wood fibers refuse to absorb any more of the liquid, I spread on a fine skim coat of solid epoxy filler to create a smooth finish surface.

Parts and Patches Are Made from the Same Wood as the Sash

Unlike fixed trim elements, a window sash is subject to a great deal of mechanical stress. To ensure that my repairs last as long as possible, I don't depend on epoxy to fill large gaps; instead, I fashion all but the smallest patches from wood. I rely on a dutchman (a patch that is made with wood) glued with an epoxy adhesive from West Systems to repair damage that would require more than a skim coat of filler (see the sidebar below).

When I have to replace an entire sash part, such as a rail or a muntin strip, I first try to scrounge up a match in a local salvage yard. But if that doesn't pan out, I can replicate the profile using a molding head cutter that fits my tablesaw. If just a portion of the original piece is damaged, I cut back to sound wood and splice new wood to old.

Whether it's a small dutchman or an entire bottom rail, every replacement part should be fashioned of the same species of wood as the sash: first-growth, tight vertical grain, if possible. I maintain a ready stock of raw material for replacement parts because I never discard any old wood.

Whenever large-scale repairs are needed, the sash has to be disassembled. Early sashes (150 years old or more) were joined by a tapered wooden peg driven through a mortise and tenon. To disassemble this type of frame, the pegs must be punched out from the small-diameter side. Don't worry about saving the pegs; they can't be reused. Sashes made in later years substituted glue for pegs; they usually can be separated by cutting through the glueline with a knife, then gently tapping the mortised section loose using a block of wood and a mallet.

After I've completed all necessary repairs, I reassemble the window sash using an exterior-grade carpenter's glue such as Titebond II® (Franklin International; 800-347-4583; www.titebond.com). Unlike an epoxy adhesive, carpenter's glue is reversible, so it allows future carpenters the opportunity to take the window apart should they ever

Glazing Takes Practice

1. To prevent breakage, I bed each pane of glass in a layer of acrylic latex caulk before I secure them with glazier's points.

2. I work glazing compound into a ³⁄₈-in.-diameter rope before pressing it into place.

3. After lubricating a putty knife with boiled linseed oil, I tool the glazing compound using my index finger as a guide. Finally, I eliminate minor imperfections in the glazing by wiping downward with a taping knife.

need to make repairs. If the joints are loose, however, I have no choice but to use a thickened epoxy adhesive to fill the gaps.

During the gluing process, the frame is squared up, then clamped tightly and allowed to set for at least 24 hours. Afterward, all surfaces are sanded thoroughly to prepare them for paint: I use 60-grit paper to knock down the high spots, followed by 100 grit to polish everything paint-grade smooth.

Preservative and Primer Ensure That the Paint Stays Stuck

Old wood presents a finishing challenge because it tends to be extremely dry. If left untreated, it will absorb the chemical binders from primer, causing early paint failure. To put some natural resins back into those dried wood fibers, I brush on a generous coating of a homemade wood preservative, a mixture of 50 percent mineral spirits and 50 percent boiled linseed oil (see the top photo on p. 110). I let the frame dry for 48 hours before priming it, but I don't use just any primer.

Traditional primers (oil or latex) soak into the wood fibers to create a bond, but they cannot soak into the epoxy patches and thus are liable to fail. Instead, I apply a coat of B-I-N® primer-sealer (Zinsser® Co. Inc.; 732-469-8100; www.zinsser.com) over all surfaces (see the bottom photo on p. 110). This product is a white shellac designed to

Old sashes need special attention before painting. After the repairs are done, the sash is treated with a generous coating of a homemade wood preservative: one-half mineral spirits, one-half boiled linseed oil (*right*). After two full days' drying time, a shellac-base primer is applied. This combination of ingredients ensures that the finish coats of paint bond to a stable, uniform surface (*bottom*).

seal knotholes, among other things, but it forms a strong surface bond that adheres equally as well to epoxy as to wood fibers.

Bed the Glass in a Bead of Caulk

Before reinstallation, I thoroughly clean all the original glass. Then I apply a fine bead of latex caulk to the shoulder that will receive the glass (see photo 1 on p. 108). I "back-putty" the glass in caulk rather than glazing compound because the supple caulk provides a cushion that lessens the chance that the fragile old glass might shatter as I'm pressing it into place. After all the panes are bedded in the sash, a few glazier's points are installed to secure the glass until the caulk has cured.

The glazing process requires finesse and a steady hand, both of which take practice to achieve (see photos 2 and 3 on pp. 108 and 109). Glazing compound does not hold paint well until it has had a couple of weeks to cure. If time allows, I store the sashes in my shop, then apply two full coats of paint before I reinstall them. When painting over the glazing compound, I've learned that it's important to let the paint overlap the glass (about $1/16$ in.); this overlap prevents water from getting behind the glazing, causing early failure.

Repaired window sashes have a greater life expectancy than new window units, but as with anything that's exposed to nature's wrath, they still have to be maintained. I urge all my clients to open and close each of their windows at least once a year and to examine their windows thoroughly for signs of rot at least every five years.

David Gibney is a restoration contractor in Smithsburg, Maryland.

Installing a Bay Window by Yourself

■ GREGORY BURR

As a general contractor with no employees, I've learned a thing or two about working alone. Getting a difficult job done by myself sometimes means I have to rent a piece of equipment or spend a few minutes making a jig. But mostly, working solo is about thinking ahead and being prepared.

Installing a bay window is a perfect example of a job that is challenging but not impossible to do alone. Bay windows are heavy, and because they hang outside the house, they need extra support both during installation and for their life span. When installing a bay window alone, I use temporary supports and prepare the window opening so that I have to lift the unit only once and don't have to hold it for long.

Make Sure the Sill Is Perfectly Level

I do a few things differently when installing a bay window alone, such as setting up a work platform. Although the window is not far off the ground, staging gives me a place to set it down close to the opening so that

Work from the Inside

When I install a bay window by myself, I frame the rough opening from the inside of the house and leave the sheathing on until just before it is time to install the window. This way, if the job takes me more than a day to complete, I don't have to worry about covering the opening to protect the house overnight.

Frame the opening, then cut the sheathing. The rough opening is framed with a header supported by jack studs and a sill that will support the window. The new framing can act as a guide for cutting the opening.

Plumb and level the framing in advance. Rather than installing the window first and then making big adjustments, shim the sill level and make one jack stud plumb before installing the window.

I don't have to hold it for too long at one time. I also use shims to make sure the sill is level and one of the jack studs on the side of the rough opening is plumb before installing the window (see the right photo above). When I lift the window into the opening and slide it toward the shimmed jack, the window shouldn't need adjustment. All I have to do is shim the top and the remaining side to fill the gap.

To lighten the window before I lift it into the rough opening by myself, I remove the two side sashes (see the photo on the facing page). Unfortunately, the center window is fixed. But by removing a few screws, I can take out the operable sashes and lighten the unit considerably. Removing the sashes also gives me access to the inside of the house through the window while I work from outside.

Remove the glass to lighten the load. It takes only a screwdriver and a few minutes to remove the operable sashes, but doing so makes lifting the window much easier.

Before installing the window, I do two things. First, I start a screw into the jamb at the location of one shim on the leveled jack stud. When I place the window in the rough opening, I drive home this screw first. The screw may need to come out or be loosened if I need to make adjustments, but it helps hold the window in the opening in the meantime. The last thing I do before setting the window in place is set up a support below the window. Scrap pieces of framing lumber cut to fit between the ground and the window work great.

Double-Check the Window before Nailing Off the Flange

Confident that I won't have to hold the heavy window for too long, I lift it into place, slide it tight against the shimmed jack stud, and secure the support underneath the window. With the support bearing most

of the window's weight, all I have to do is steady the unit while I drive in the waiting screw. At this point I also drive 1½-in. roofing nails into the top corners of the window flange. But I don't drive in the nails completely. I leave them out just enough so that I will be able to pull them easily if I need to make an adjustment. With the window temporarily secured, I double-check the bottom of the unit for level and the side of the unit for plumb. It is important that the unit be installed perfectly so that the casement windows open and close properly. If the unit is perfect, I set the nails into the top corners of the flange. If not, I adjust the window from the inside with more shims.

Before nailing the side flanges, I use a straightedge to check that the jambs are not bowed in the middle. The edge of the side sash where it meets the center unit is held straight by the fixed center window, but the edges that meet the house can bow and cause problems. Once I am sure the edges are not bowed, I nail the flange with 1½-in. roofing nails every 8 in.

To keep out water, I seal around the entire window with silicone caulk, then lay housewrap over the side flanges. I then secure the housewrap to the side and bottom flanges with contractor's tape (the kind used to seal housewrap). Above the window, I will build a roof that is flashed separately to keep water from leaking in.

Inside the house, I shim each side of the window in three places: the center, a few inches from the bottom corner, and a few inches from the top corner. Shims should be used to form a tight, flat surface that fills the gap between the window and the studs and provides a place to secure the window with screws. If the window jamb moves when I drive in the screws, the shims are not tight enough. Before I trim around the inside of the window, I stuff strips of fiberglass insulation between the shims.

When you're by yourself, scaffolding is better than a ladder. With the support leg and installation screw ready, I lift the window onto the scaffold and then into the opening.

Have temporary support ready. Below the window, a temporary support made from scrap lumber bears the weight of the window until it is secured.

Start a screw before lifting. A screw or nail partially set into the jamb will make life easier when you lift the window into the opening and need to secure the unit quickly.

The Roof Protects the Window and Helps Support It

There are companies that sell factory-made roofs for bay windows. But when I install a bay window, I build the roof myself to be sure it offers both protection and support. I build a 45-degree hip roof with 2x4 rafters and plywood sheathing. I also add a soffit and fascia to the top of the window to create an overhang that protects the glass from water dripping off the roof.

To make sure the roof is helping support the window, I first glue and screw a 2x4 plate to the perimeter of the top of the window (see the top left photo on p. 116). The 2x4s give me extra blocking on the window to which I screw the rafters for a strong hold. From the blocking, the rafters extend up to the house, where I screw them secure-

Lift the window onto the support. There is no need to muscle the window into the opening in one shot. Lift it onto the temporary support and ease it from there into position.

Secure the window to the plumb stud. Slide the window against the prepared jack stud and fasten the waiting screw. The winvdow is now secure enough to be left alone while the installation is completed.

ly to framing members. The rafters frame the roof and prevent the top of the window from pulling away from the house.

I fit a piece of rigid-foam insulation inside the 2x4s and on the top of the window. On most 45-degree bay windows, all I need to frame the roof are two common rafters, two side ledger rafters, two hip rafters, and ½-in. plywood for sheathing.

If water gets inside the roof, it will rot the window and likely get into the wall cavity,

so I pay a lot of attention to flashing the roof. I use copper drip edge to prevent water from wicking up underneath the shingles, an ice-and-water barrier that covers the entire roof and extends onto the wall, step flashing that goes up the side of the roof with each course of shingles, and base flashing along the top of the roof.

Screw 2x4 plates to the top of the window for strength. The roof helps hold the window in the opening, so there needs to be a good place to attach the rafters. The 2x4 plate also makes it easy to create an overhang to protect the window from dripping water.

Rigid foam insulates the bottom. A piece of foam insulation and ½-in. plywood cut to the shape of the window help prevent heat loss below the large window. Decorative brackets add the final level of support.

Add Insulation and Support below the Window

Before I install brackets below the window, I cut another piece of rigid-foam insulation and a piece of ½-in. plywood to seal the bottom of the window (see the bottom photo above). I use adhesive between the layers to help hold the plywood and foam to the window, and I hide the assembly with trim.

The last step is to add brackets that decorate and help support the window from below. Metal brackets can be hidden behind the siding, but I prefer to use decorative wood brackets (www.vintagewoodworks.com). I attach the brackets to the window and to the house, again making sure to screw into framing members.

Gregory Burr is a general contractor in Westbrook, Connecticut.

New Window in an Old Wall

■ RICK ARNOLD

A friend of mine recently had his appendix removed. Three tiny incisions, the right tools, and the right procedures, and he was back on his feet just hours after an operation that used to send a patient into weeks of recovery. Home-remodeling projects can be similar. Careful planning can keep cutting and demolition to a minimum with little disruption to the living environment and the lives of the clients. And the job takes less time.

One such project is putting a new window into an existing home (see the photo at right). I try to perform most of the work from the outside, leaving the wallboard intact as an interior barrier against the mess, right up until the window goes in.

Upgrade with minimal mess. A new window improved the look and let in light. Working from the outside controlled the mess.

1. Strip Off the Siding

You'll be happy if the house has vinyl siding: It comes off easily. Available at most hardware stores, a zipper slips between siding panels to separate them.

After lifting the upper panel, a flat bar pops the nails of the siding panel below.

Siding in the window area comes off first. With the tool below, vinyl siding is one of the easiest types to remove and replace.

Peel Back the Skin

The first step is to remove the siding in the area where the window is going to be located (see the photos above). If another window is on the same wall, I use it to gauge the head height for the new window. I also check around the corner to make sure that the new window will be at the same elevation as any existing window that's in the same room (because you never know).

I remove the siding, starting with the course above the window location and moving down to a course or two below the window. Because this particular house had vinyl siding, I knew I'd be removing full lengths of siding and exposing a large horizontal area, so I didn't have to be to fussy about the horizontal location at this point. If I had been working with sidewall shingles or with clapboards, I would have needed to be more precise about locating the window and

With all the siding removed, the housewrap is peeled back to reveal the wall sheathing underneath.

removing just a small area of siding around the spot of the new window.

To unlock the top row of vinyl, I use a tool called a zipper, basically a flat hook that is inserted behind the interlocking edges of two adjacent pieces. The tool grabs the lip of the top piece of vinyl and bends it out, unlocking it from the lower piece. Once the work has started, pulling the tool along the length of the siding separates the two pieces, opening them up like a zipper.

With the top piece of vinyl lifted up, I pull out the nails from the lower one. When all the nails are removed, I grasp the length of siding and push down, unsnapping it from the next course. The remainder of the siding is removed easily in the same fashion. Next, I carefully cut the housewrap and tack it out of the way until the opening is framed.

2. Lay Out the New Window Opening

Use existing framing if possible for part of the rough opening.

With the sheathing exposed, the sides of the rough opening are laid out first. In this case, an existing stud forms the left side of the opening, and the author measures over for the right side.

The top of the opening matches a window on the same wall.

Mark the Opening on the Sheathing

With the wall sheathing exposed, I now can locate and mark the rough opening precisely (see the left and center photos above). The existing stud locations are easy to determine by the nail patterns, and on this job the rough opening fell about 2 in. away from the edge of a stud.

To make life a little easier, I try to use existing studs for the sides of the rough opening, as long as the studs are close to plumb. (If they are way out of plumb, I adjust the opening to miss them completely and insert new plumb studs for both sides.) To land the opening on a stud, I had permission from the owner to move the window one way or the other, up to 6 in. In this case, I moved the opening about 2 in. until it fell along the edge of a stud. Using that edge as a start-

Protective covering installed by the local utility company (see tip below)

The bottom is measured down from the top point.

A circular saw with the blade set at a shallow depth cuts the sheathing.

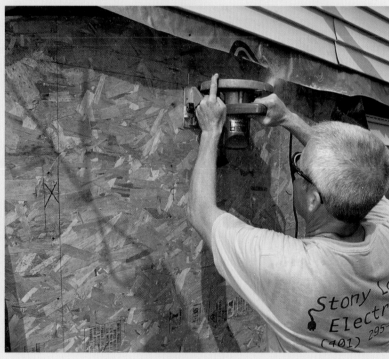

ing point, I drew the rest of the rough opening on the sheathing.

Cut the Sheathing First, Then the Studs

Because this wall happened to be a gable end, I didn't have to install a load-bearing header and jack studs, which meant that I didn't have to take out a large section of sheathing. Using a circular saw with the blade set slightly deeper than the thickness of the sheathing, I cut and remove the sheathing from the opening. I set the blade shallow to avoid hitting anything that may be buried in the wall.

With the sheathing removed, I cut the exposed insulation just below the sill height and remove it from the bays, except the bay where I'm going to add a full-height stud. For that bay, I remove the full batt of insulation, cut it to be about 1 in. shy of the verti-

TIP

If your work is anywhere near electrical wires, your local utility company will install a protective covering to keep you safe (see the center photo above).

3. Prep the Opening from the Outside

Leave room for the sills when you remove the studs.

A reciprocating saw plunged through the sheathing 1½ in. below the opening cuts the stud at the right height for the sill.

With the old studs removed, screws attach the new framing to minimize wall damage inside.

New header and sill pieces go into the recess left by the reciprocating saw.

cal edge of the sheathing, and replace it in the wall cavity.

If the header and sill are just 2x4s on flat, I mark the sheathing 1½ in. up from the top of the opening and 1½ in. down from the bottom at each stud location (see the photos at right on p. 121 and the photos above).

With a reciprocating saw, I plunge-cut through the sheathing and then through the full depth of the studs at my marks. I don't worry if the blade pokes through the drywall a little. The interior treatment should cover any place the blade might pierce through.

Once the studs are cut, I knock the pieces out of the opening carefully with a hammer.

New Framing Slips behind the Sheathing

Because I used an existing stud for the left side of the opening, I had to insert a new stud only for the right side. For this stud I cut a length of 2x4 to go from the sole plate to the top plate.

I slide the new stud into the wall cavity, and then, starting at the bottom, I tap the stud gently into position. I fasten the studs in place by driving deck screws through the sheathing as well as through the stud and into the plates, if I can reach. Driving screws causes less vibration than nailing and minimizes the chance for drywall cracks inside. With the stud fastened securely, I replace any pieces of sheathing that had been removed for sliding the stud into the wall.

The next step is cutting and replacing the insulation in the newly formed stud bays above the 2x4 header and below the sill. After that, I measure, cut, and install the header and sill. As with the new stud, I screw the header and sill to the sheathing and toe-screw them into the support studs.

With the framing complete, I can take out the wallboard that has been protecting the inside of the house (see the photos at right). To mark the wallboard for cutting, I drive a nail through each corner of the framed opening from the outside. Inside the house, I draw lines connecting the nail holes to outline the opening.

To keep the gypsum dust to a minimum, I use my cordless trim saw with an old carbide blade to cut right through the wallboard with little effort. Its relatively slow blade speed creates no more gypsum dust than cutting by hand. After I cut and remove the wallboard, I screw the perimeter of the opening to the new framing.

4. Wallboard Comes Out

Drywall on the inside protects against construction mess on the outside.

Inside, the corners are connected and the opening is drawn.

Nails driven into the corners from the outside transfer the opening to the inside.

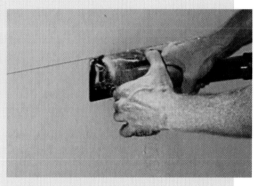

A trim saw with a carbide blade cuts the wallboard with minimal mess.

The slow blade speed of the Makita 9.6v circular saw (800-462-5482) lets it cut drywall without making a lot of dust.

The wallboard comes out, making way for the new window.

If you've done your work carefully, putting in the window is the easiest part.

Installing the window is an anticlimax after all the careful prep work. The window height again is measured down from the siding course to match the neighboring window.

Flashing and housewrap are woven back around the window and under the siding.

The siding is reinstalled and zipped back in place.

Installing the Window and Buttoning Up

With the rough opening complete inside and out, my attention turns to the window itself. The installation and flashing are the same as with a normal window. For this window, I cut and bent aluminum flashing for the sill and used flashing membrane to seal the corners.

Making sure the head of the window lines up with its neighbor down the wall is easier with a helper (see the left photo above). The crew member inside simply shims the window to the right height, while the outside crew member measures down from the siding course above.

After the window is nailed in place, one crew member tackles the inside finish around the window. The crew member outside completes the flashing around the window and then reinstalls the siding. When the last row of siding has been nailed on, the zipper tool is used in reverse to mate together the rows of siding, and after four hours' work, the window looks as if it had always been there.

Rick Arnold, a contributing editor to Fine Homebuilding, *is a contractor and residential consultant in North Kingstown, Rhode Island, and the author of* Working with Concrete *(The Taunton Press, 2003).*

Installing Vinyl-Clad Windows

■ RICK ARNOLD AND MIKE GUERTIN

There are many significant milestones during a home-building project: first tree to fall, first scoop of earth, final roof rafter set, etc. But one of our favorites is window-installation day. For us, it's usually the day the bank designates the house as a "weathertight shell" and then issues the corresponding check. But even with that added incentive, we never rush the process of installing windows. The last thing a builder needs is a callback to fix a leaky window.

Check the Flanges before Installation

The windows we install most often are vinyl-clad, meaning they have a wooden frame wrapped with a protective layer of vinyl. Depending on the manufacturer and on the type of window, vinyl-clad windows have either an integral flange that is part of the extrusion covering the wood frame of the window or a flange that friction-fits into a slot on the head and sides of the window frame. The vinyl-clad double-hung windows we installed on this project were the slotted type.

Make way for the flanges. When the window opening is cut in the housewrap, 2-in. slits are made beside the opening for the window flanges to slide through.

Head flange slips under the housewrap. As the window is lifted into position, the outside crew member guides the head flange under the housewrap at the top of the opening.

The windows may be shipped without the flanges attached, or the flanges may have come loose during shipping. So we check all the windows to make sure the flanges are attached properly before we begin installation. To reattach the flanges, we first press them into the slot by hand. Once they're in position, we drive them home using a 1x block set against the inward lip of the flange to cushion our hammer blows.

Flanges Tuck under the Housewrap

We usually start thinking about window installation before the excavator takes that first scoop of earth for the foundation. As the windows are chosen for each location in the house, model numbers and rough-opening sizes are noted. All these numbers are double-checked as the house is being framed.

We use housewrap as a secondary drainage plane. So instead of cutting the window openings diagonally from the upper corners, we cut straight across the top of the opening.

The bottom and sides of the housewrap are cut and stapled into the sides of the framed opening in the usual fashion. But we leave the top loose with no staples for at least 2 in. above the opening where the head flange of the window tucks under the wrap. Next, we extend the top cut about 2 in. out from the opening on each side for the side flanges to slide through (see the bottom photo on p. 125). As the housewrap is cut and stapled to the opening, we also check for protruding nails or anything else that could interfere with installation.

Two Crew Members Make Installation Easier

We've found that the quickest, safest way to install windows is with two crew members, one inside and one outside the house. Inside duties include handing the window out the opening, centering it, and adjusting it in the opening as the crew member on the outside directs. The outside crew member levels, plumbs, and squares the window and then fastens it to the wall.

Before lifting a window into position, we like to unlock and raise the lower sash to give us a better handhold. The crew member on the inside then passes the window unit out through the opening top first, angling it slightly to clear the opening. Having both sash up makes the unit top-heavy, so we take extra care handling it.

As the window is lifted into the rough opening, the outside crew member tips the top toward the house and guides the head flange under the housewrap with the side flanges passing through the two slits made earlier (see the top photo on p. 125). Once the head flange is under the wrap, the window is lifted up and in. For the lift, the inside crew member, who must be on sure footing, is responsible for the weight of the window, while the outside crew member balances it and guides it into position.

Don't Let Go of That Window

Once the bottom of the window is pulled into the opening and is resting on the rough sill, the inside crew member hands the level out and gets ready to adjust the window in the opening. The weight of the window makes it want to fall out the opening, so whenever one of the crew members needs to release his hold to grab a tool or to make an adjustment, he lets his partner know. That way, the window is never left unsupported.

Center the window first. The outside crew member holds the window in place while the window is centered in its opening from the inside.

At this point, the inside crew member centers the window side to side in the opening with a flat bar (see the photo above). The outside crew member then sets the level on top of the window (see the top photo at right) and directs the crew member inside to lift the low side with the flat bar until the unit is level. A shim shingle is then slipped between the bottom of the jamb and the rough sill to keep the window level until the outside can be nailed at the tops of the side flanges (see the bottom photo at right).

Every window we've installed has called for either 1¾-in. or 2-in. galvanized roofing nails or other broad-head nails to be used as fasteners. After the upper corners of the side flanges have been nailed (see the left photo on p. 128), we recheck the level to make sure nothing drifted.

Two sides of window installation. A level is held outside on the head of the window (*above*), and instructions are given to the inside crew member to shim the window as needed (*left*).

Top corners are first to be nailed.
When the window is centered and the head is leveled, the nails are driven in the top corners to hold the top of the window in place.

Plumb jamb. No, not a breakfast spread. The inside crew member moves the window side to side with a flat bar as instructed by the outside crew member who holds a level against the jambs.

Check for square before nailing off the bottom corners. A measuring tape is stretched from corner to corner, and diagonal measurements are taken to make sure the window is square in its opening.

We intentionally avoid nailing the top flange at this point because with its friction fit into the head jamb, the flange could pull out while we're adjusting the sides for plumb in the next operation. Windows with integral flanges can be nailed at the top left and right corners without a problem.

Get the Sides Plumb and Square

Next, the inside crew member adjusts the bottom of the window side to side with a flat bar, while outside, a level is held against the window jamb (see the center photo above).

When the jamb reads plumb, the outside crew member drives a single nail at the bot-tom of the side flange without driving the nail home. The other jamb is then checked for plumb, and another nail is driven to secure the last corner of the window.

Before driving the two bottom nails home, we measure the window diagonally from corner to corner to make sure it's square (see the right photo above). Leveling the top and plumbing the sides of the window should make it square, but the diagonal measurements are the best confirmation that the window is square. Once we're satisfied, we set the bottom nails.

We straighten the side jambs by using a straightedge (see the left photo on the facing page) or by checking the reveal between the sash and the jamb by eye. The middles

A straightedge ensures smooth window operation. After the corners of the window are nailed in, a straightedge is placed against the jamb (*left*), and a nail is driven to hold the jamb straight (*above*). A straight jamb is essential for the sash to slide up and down properly.

ere in Rhode Island, ocean-front properties are in big demand, so we regularly find ourselves working within a stone's throw of the ocean. During the frequent storms that buffet the coast, rain rarely falls down from the sky; it blows in sideways.

In this environment, standard weatherproofing details do little more than channel wind-driven water into building assemblies. And leaks are most likely to occur around the windows.

The first thing we learned is to stop relying on caulk. Sun, wind, and water all conspire to penetrate even 50-year sealants in just a few months. Instead, we assume that wind-driven water will find its way in, despite our best efforts. Our strategy, then, is to make sure any water that makes it past our defenses is directed back to the outside.

Slope the Rough Sill

The details to redirect leaks occur before the windows arrive. First, we oversize the rough-opening height by ¼ in. during framing and install housewrap as we do for a standard installation.

At the bottom of the opening, we install a piece of 6-in.-wide clapboard with the thick edge toward the inside of the wall (see photo 1). The clapboard gives us a sill with a slight pitch.

We make the window drainage pan of adhesive-backed bituminous membrane (see photo 2). We cut a 9-in.-wide strip of membrane about 1 ft. longer than the width of the opening. The membrane is pressed onto the clapboard, with 6 in. or so of membrane run up the inside of each jack stud.

Next, we make a diagonal cut in the membrane starting ½ in. out from the bottom corners to create two flaps. But before we fold the

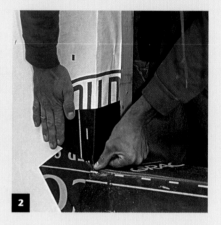

of the jambs are often bowed in or out and have to be straight for the window to slide in the jamb easily without being loose. After the jambs are straightened and secured with a nail (see the right photo on p. 129), the inside crew member checks the sash operation, then lowers and locks the bottom sash and checks the margins.

By the way, some window companies ship their windows with a plastic strap to keep the jambs from spreading during installation. We leave those straps in place until the jambs are shimmed and insulated.

Don't Skimp on the Nails

The process to this point takes about 10 minutes. Finishing installation typically takes another 10 minutes. But rather than have the inside crew member waiting around all that time, both crew members usually move on to the next window until all the windows are secured in place. Then one or both crew members can nail off all the windows.

All the window brands we use have nail holes prepunched in the flanges. The recommended nail spacing varies, so we check each manufacturer's instructions before nailing off. This brand calls for nails every flaps onto the walls, we press 6-in. by 6-in. pieces of membrane onto the outside wall to span the corners between the membrane flaps. We stick the filler pieces onto the wall so that the pan material overlaps onto them to form a leakproof corner.

The bituminous membrane is pressed tightly into all the corners to prevent a void that could puncture during window installation. On cold days, the membrane may not stick well to the sheathing or to the housewrap, but a few staples will hold it in place until the adhesive activates.

Seal the Flanges with Bituminous Membrane

We install the window as we do in a standard installation, except that we slit the housewrap 6 in. at the top corners rather than 2 in. Instead of using tape to seal window to housewrap, we seal the sides of the window to the housewrap with 6-in.-wide strips of membrane. The side strips extend through the slits and then stick to the wall sheathing under the housewrap.

For the head of the window, we slip a 6-in. strip of membrane under the housewrap (see photo 3). The head strip covers the top window flange and extends over the side strips. We let the side strips extend down over the pan flashing. As added insurance, we tape the housewrap to the membrane along the head of the window and out beyond the horizontal slit (see photo 4).

The bottom flap is again held in place by the siding so that any water that reaches the pan can drain out. By the way, this window-installation detail works great under vinyl siding. Vinyl siding is leakier than other sidings, so it can use some help to keep water out of walls.

6 in. to 8 in. Their holes are punched at 4 in. apart, so we drive nails at every other hole.

When nailing off the head flange, we lift the flap of housewrap rather than nailing through it (see the left photo on p. 132). We always take special care when nailing off vinyl flanges, especially in cold weather when they can become brittle and crack easily.

On occasion, we've tried speeding up the nailing process by using pneumatic coil-roofing nailers. We're usually pretty good at hitting the prepunched holes. But missing with the pneumatic nailer can cause flange cracks, so we prefer to spend the extra time hand-nailing the flanges.

Most window manufacturers wrap flanges all the way around their windows. However, this brand has a soft, flexible flap at the bottom rather than a rigid flange. We tack down this flap with a couple of staples.

Housewrap Tape Seals the Windows

Window installation isn't complete until we've taped the window flanges to the housewrap. Taping the flanges helps prevent rainwater from entering the wall cavity, and it draftproofs the building envelope.

We first tape the sides where the flanges are on top of the housewrap. We extend the tape beyond the slits that we made for

Tape air-seals the window. As a final measure, the flanges are taped to the housewrap. At the head of the window, the housewrap is taped to the window flange (*top*). The flexible flange at the bottom of the window is taped to the housewrap (*bottom*).

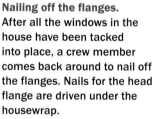

Nailing off the flanges. After all the windows in the house have been tacked into place, a crew member comes back around to nail off the flanges. Nails for the head flange are driven under the housewrap.

the top flange and then run tape across the head of the window where the flange is underneath the housewrap (see the top right photo above).

In the past, we've treated the bottom flange two different ways. If the installation includes the drainage pan that we use in rough-weather situations (see the sidebar on p. 130), then we omit the tape to permit any water that might get behind the window flanges to drain out. But for our standard installation, we tape the bottom flange to the housewrap to complete the air seal around the window (see the bottom right photo above).

Notes on Other Flanged Windows

Installation of casement and awning-flanged windows is nearly identical to the process we use for double hungs. The biggest difference is that we don't open the windows during handling. With the sash open, they become awkward, and their jambs tend to rack.

Another installation difference is that we boost the window units off the sills with thin (³⁄₁₆ in. to ¼ in.) blocks under the corners. These blocks give us space between the unit and the rough framing at the bottom to spray in air-sealing foam later. Other than that, the processes are identical.

Rick Arnold and Mike Guertin, contributing editors to Fine Homebuilding, *are builders and construction consultants in North Kingstown and East Greenwich, Rhode Island.*

Dressing Up Stock Windows

■ SCOTT MCBRIDE

Mark Leas owns a thriving millwork business in the nation's capital, specializing in high-end commercial interiors. Flawless bookmatched paneling and 8-in. crown moldings are all in a day's work.

When the time came to build his own house, Leas was disappointed in the limited exterior-trim choices offered by even the best window manufacturers. The aluminum or vinyl-clad options didn't mesh with the Georgian detailing of his new home. When it came to primed wood casings, most manufacturers proposed to trim their windows with rot-prone finger-jointed white pine. Leas was building this house to last, using premium materials such as redwood siding and copper flashing. He didn't want to replace rotted window trim 10 years down the road.

All the Molding Is Back-Primed to Extend Its Life

Faced with these options, Leas bought aluminum-clad Pella windows (800-547-3552) that attach to the house with nailing fins. He then milled his own trim from rot-resistant Honduras mahogany (see the photo at right).

New windows frequently lack the stylish casings of their predecessors. Applied moldings can dress stock windows to fit just about any style of architecture.

Moldings Add Detail to Stock Windows

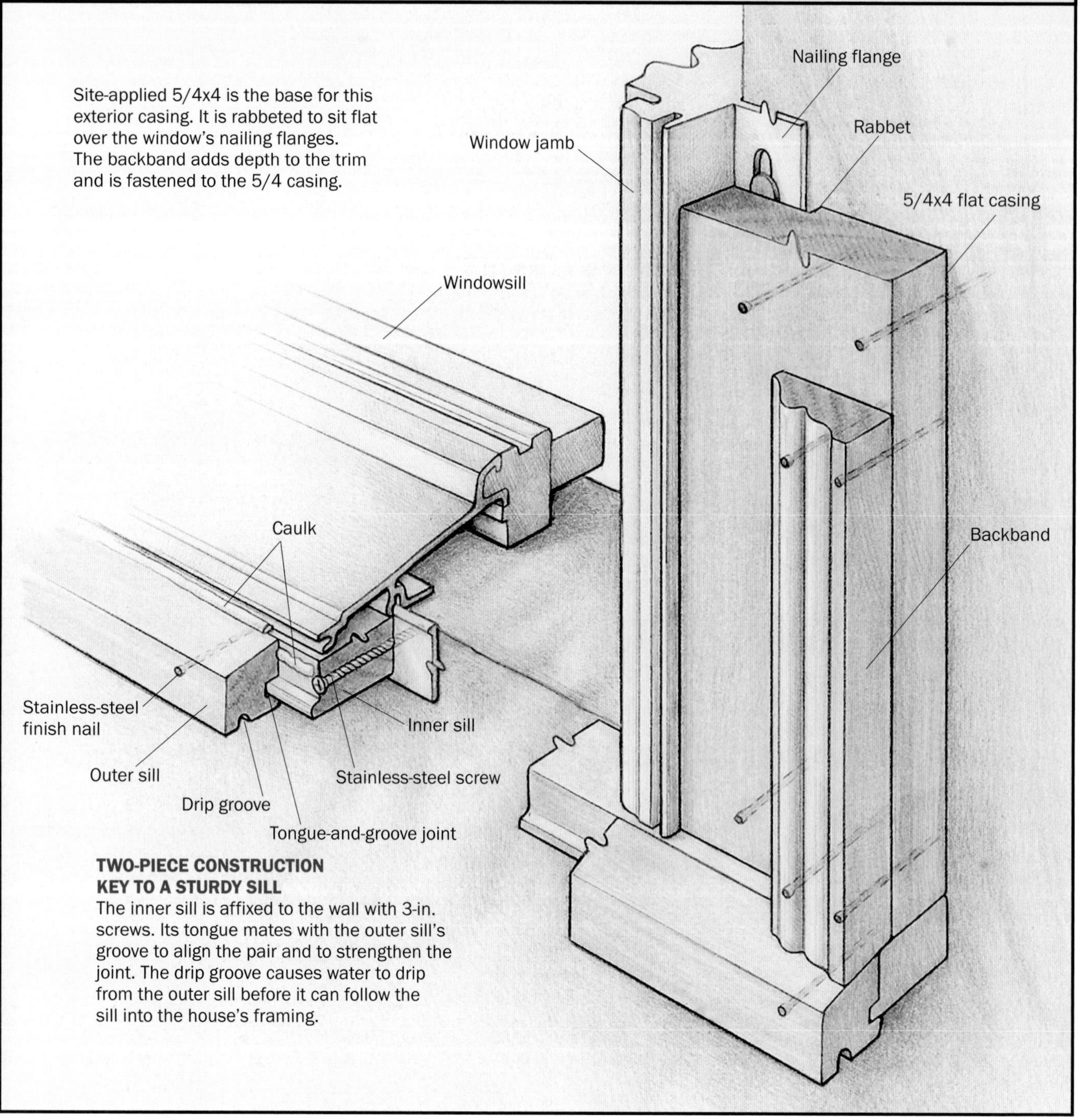

Site-applied 5/4x4 is the base for this exterior casing. It is rabbeted to sit flat over the window's nailing flanges. The backband adds depth to the trim and is fastened to the 5/4 casing.

Nailing flange

Window jamb

Rabbet

5/4x4 flat casing

Windowsill

Backband

Caulk

Stainless-steel finish nail

Outer sill

Inner sill

Stainless-steel screw

Drip groove

Tongue-and-groove joint

TWO-PIECE CONSTRUCTION KEY TO A STURDY SILL
The inner sill is affixed to the wall with 3-in. screws. Its tongue mates with the outer sill's groove to align the pair and to strengthen the joint. The drip groove causes water to drip from the outer sill before it can follow the sill into the house's framing.

The trim consists of a two-piece sill and a flat casing topped with a backband that's shaped similar to lumberyard rake molding (see the drawings above). The flat 5/4x4 casing is rabbeted 1/8 in. deep along its inner edge to accommodate the window's nailing fins. All the material was alkyd-primed on four sides before delivery to the job.

Leas's cigar-smoking band of Irish carpenters applied the trim at the job site, starting by holding the casing legs in place against the windows and marking their length. Their tops were mitered, and the legs were nailed home with 3-in. stainless-steel finish nails.

With the legs in place, the carpenters measured and cut the sills and head casings to length (see the top photo at right). Installing the head casing was simple: The carpenters caulked the mating surfaces of the miters with acrylic caulk, then nailed the heads to the wall.

Two-Piece Sill Is Sturdy

To extend beyond the combined depth of the casing and backband, the sill had to be 2¼ in. wide. Efficiently and discreetly attaching such a wide sill to the building was tricky.

Leas's solution was a two-piece sill with a tongue-and-groove joint that aligns and strengthens the assembly. The square inner sill snugs up tightly below the window. It is first nailed to the bottoms of the casing legs (see the center photo at right); then stainless-steel screws pull it against the sidewall. Next, 15-ga. finish nails fasten the outer sill to the inner (see the bottom photo at right). The resulting two-piece assembly has the strength of screws without the tedium of screw holes to plug. To keep out water, a bead of caulk is run between the two sill pieces before they're nailed together.

The outer sill's top is beveled to shed water. Caulk seals the joint between this sill and the window. A drip groove milled in the sill's bottom defeats capillary action by causing water that follows the sill's surface to drip off. The outer sill hangs ¼ in. below the inner, giving the chunky look of a 2-in.-thick sill and sheltering the siding that tucks below. Finally, the backband was nailed on flush with the outer edge of the casing. To finish, a copper drip cap covers the head.

Scott McBride *is a contributing editor to* Fine Homebuilding.

Trimming around the Window

The casing legs have been cut and nailed to the house. Precise measurements can now be taken for the sill and head.

The inner sill is nailed to the casing legs. Next, the carpenters will use stainless-steel screws to affix the inner sill to the house.

Finish nails hold the outer sill to the inner. Caulk applied between the two sill pieces before nailing seals out water.

Understanding Energy-Efficient Windows

■ PAUL FISETTE

A respected builder I know told me how he learned the true value of energy-efficient windows. In the course of his business, he installed a builder's line of windows from a well-known manufacturer in every house he built. He felt good about his choice; he purchased the windows from a manufacturer with a reputation for quality, but they cost 10 percent less than the same manufacturer's standard line of low-e, argon-filled windows, saving him about $600* per house. He even put them in his own new home. The first winter he lived there, though, he noticed that the windows seemed cold. Only then did he compare the U-values with the same manufacturer's standard windows. He did some math and concluded that his windows were costing

Radiant heat lost through windows can be reduced by placing low-e coatings on glass that reflect specific wavelengths of energy.

Windows Lose Heat in Four Ways

The rate at which a window loses heat through the combination of the four is called its U-value. It is the inverse of the R-value, so the lower the U-value, the greater the insulative value of the window.

1. Conduction is the direct transfer of heat through the window to the outdoors.

2. Radiation is the movement of heat as infrared energy through the glass.

3. Convection occurs when air gives up its heat to the cooler glass and sinks toward the floor. This movement sucks new, warmer air toward the glass that is in turn cooled, creating a draft.

4. Air leakage is the passage of heated air through cracks and around weatherstripping.

Low-e Glass Reflects Heat Energy while Admitting Visible Light

This keeps heat out during the summer and during the winter. In the winter, low-angle visible light passes into the house and is absorbed by the home's interior.

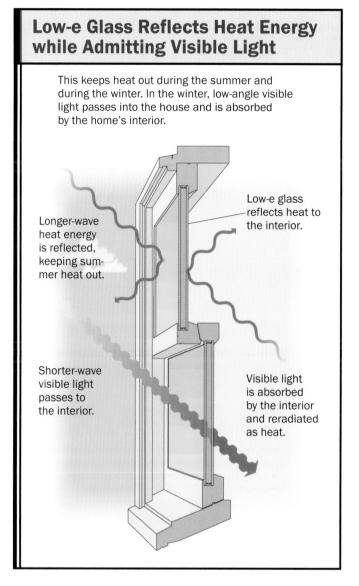

Longer-wave heat energy is reflected, keeping summer heat out.

Low-e glass reflects heat to the interior.

Shorter-wave visible light passes to the interior.

Visible light is absorbed by the interior and reradiated as heat.

---

him about $150 a year. By his estimation, the low-e windows would have paid for themselves in four years and made his home more comfortable for their entire life span.

My friend based his conclusions on widely accepted averages; and although certainly not exact, they were probably not far off the mark. Experiences such as his are common, yet they are easily avoidable with a basic understanding of how energy-efficient windows work. When you choose new windows, appearance is often the first consideration. Initial cost is the next issue: Which window within the favored style costs the least? But liking a window's appearance is a fuzzy proposition, and cost really depends on durability and on the

energy dollars pumped through the windows each year (see the chart on p. 138). I am convinced that if we could see energy loss as we see color and shape, energy performance would top the list of window considerations.

Windows are thermal holes. An average home may lose 30 percent of its heat or air-conditioning energy through its windows. Energy-efficient windows save money each and every month. There are even some cases where new windows can be net energy gainers. The payback period for selecting energy-efficient units ranges from 2 years to 10 years. In new construction, their higher initial cost can be offset because you'll probably need a smaller, less expensive heating and cooling system. And more-durable

WINDOW CHOICE HAS A REAL EFFECT ON HEATING AND COOLING COSTS. This chart is based on a computer model of heating costs for a 1,540-sq.-ft. house with R-30 ceiling insulation and R-19 in the walls and floor. The window area is equal to 15 percent of the floor area.

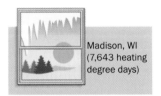

Madison, WI
(7,643 heating
degree days)

St. Louis, MO
(4,948 heating
degree days)

Phoenix, AZ
(1,444 heating
degree days)

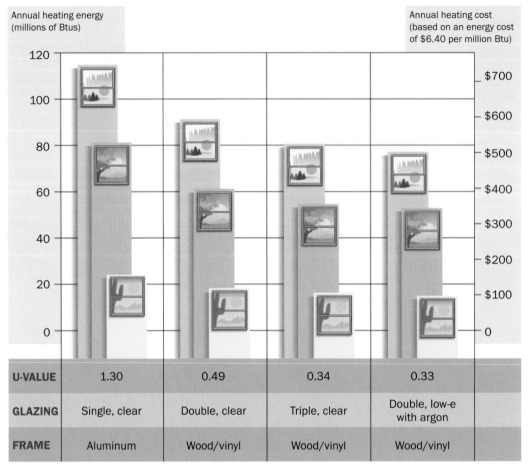

Annual heating energy
(millions of Btus)

Annual heating cost
(based on an energy cost
of $6.40 per million Btu)

U-VALUE	1.30	0.49	0.34	0.33
GLAZING	Single, clear	Double, clear	Triple, clear	Double, low-e with argon
FRAME	Aluminum	Wood/vinyl	Wood/vinyl	Wood/vinyl

windows may cost less in the long haul because of lowered maintenance and replacement costs. Plus, you'll be more comfortable the whole while you live with them.

Keeping Heat In (or Out)

Windows lose and gain heat by conduction, convection, radiation, and air leakage (see the left drawing on p. 137). This heat transfer is expressed with U-values, or U-factors. U-values are the mathematical inverse of R-values. So an R-value of 2 equals a U-value of ½, or 0.5. Unlike R-values, lower U-value indicates higher insulating value.

Conduction is the movement of heat through a solid material. Touch a hot skillet, and you feel heat conducted from the stove through the pan. Heat flows through a window much the same way. With a less conductive material, you impede heat flow. Multiple-glazed windows trap low-conductance gas such as argon between panes of glass. Thermally resistant edge spacers and window frames reduce conduction, too.

Convection is another way heat moves through windows. In a cold climate, heated indoor air rubs against the interior surface of window glass. The air cools, becomes more dense and drops toward the floor. As the stream of air drops, warm air rushes in to take its place at the glass surface. The cycle, a convective loop, is self-perpetuating. You recognize this movement as a cold draft and turn up the heat. Unfortunately, each 1°F increase in thermostat setting increases energy use 2 percent. Multiple panes of glass separated by low-conductance gas fillings and warm edge spacers, combined

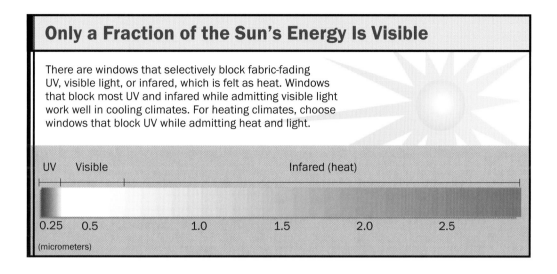

Only a Fraction of the Sun's Energy Is Visible

There are windows that selectively block fabric-fading UV, visible light, or infared, which is felt as heat. Windows that block most UV and infared while admitting visible light work well in cooling climates. For heating climates, choose windows that block UV while admitting heat and light.

| UV | Visible | | Infared (heat) | | | |

| 0.25 | 0.5 | 1.0 | 1.5 | 2.0 | 2.5 |

(micrometers)

with thermally resistant frames, raise inboard glass temperatures, slow convection, and improve comfort.

Radiant transfer is the movement of heat as long-wave heat energy from a warmer body to a cooler body. Radiant transfer is the warm feeling on your face when you stand near a woodstove. Conversely, your face feels cool when it radiates its heat to a cold sheet of window glass. But radiant-heat loss is more than a perception. Clear glass absorbs heat and reradiates it outdoors. Radiant-heat loss through windows can be greatly reduced by placing low-e coatings on glass that reflect specific wavelengths of energy (see the right drawing on p. 137). In the same way, low-e coatings keep the summer heat out.

Air leakage siphons about half of an average home's heating and cooling energy to the outdoors. Air leakage through windows is responsible for much of this loss. Well-designed windows have durable weatherstripping and high-quality closing devices that effectively block air leakage. Hinged windows such as casements and awnings clamp more tightly against weatherstripping than do double-hung windows. But the difference is slight; well-made double-hungs are acceptable. How well the individual pieces of the window unit are joined

together also affects air leakage. Glass-to-frame, frame-to-frame, and sash-to-frame connections must be tight. The technical specifications for windows list values for air leakage as cubic feet per minute (cfm) per square foot/ft² of window. Look for windows with certified air-leakage rates of less than 0.30 cfm/ft². Lowest values are best.

Letting In the Right Amount of Sun

In a cold climate, we welcome the sun's heat and light most of the time. And once we capture the heat, we don't want to give it up. In a warm climate, we don't want the heat, but we do want the light. Advances in window technology let us have it both ways.

Less than half of the sun's energy is visible (see the chart above). Longer wavelengths—beyond the red part of the visible spectrum—are infrared, which is felt as heat. Shorter wavelengths, beyond purple, are ultraviolet (UV). When the sun's energy strikes a window, visible light, heat, and UV are either reflected, absorbed, or transmitted into the building.

Enter low-e glass coatings, transparent metallic oxides that reflect up to 90 percent of long-wave heat energy, while passing shorter wave, visible light. In hot climates,

TIP

Besides giving you a nice view, high-visible trans-mittance windows can save energy because you need less artificial light.

they reflect the sun's long-wave heat energy while admitting visible light, thereby keeping the house cooler in the summer. And in cold climates, they reflect long-wave radiant heat back into the house, again while admitting visible light. This shorter wavelength visible light is absorbed by floors, walls and furniture. It reradiates from them as long-wave heat energy that the reflective, low-e coating keeps inside. Low-e coatings work best in heating climates when applied to the internal, or interpane, surface of the interior pane. Conversely, in cooling climates, low-e coatings work best applied to the interpane surface of the exterior pane.

Low-e coatings improve the insulating value of a window roughly as much as adding an additional pane of glass does. And combining low-e coatings with low-conductance gas fillings, such as argon or krypton, boosts energy efficiency by nearly 100 percent over clear glass. Argon and krypton are safe, inert gases, and they will leak from the window over time. Studies suggest a 10 percent loss over the course of 20 years, but that will reduce the U-value of the unit by only a few percent. The added cost for low-e coatings and low-conductance gas fillings is only about 5 percent of the window's overall cost. It's a no-brainer.

Taking in the View

Windows with high visible transmittance (VT) are easy to see through and admit natural daylight. Besides giving you a nice view, high-VT windows can save energy because you need less artificial light. Some tints and coatings that block heat also reduce visible transmission, so be careful. Manufacturers list the VTs of windows as comparisons with the amount of visible light that would pass through an open hole in the wall the same size as the window. VT is sometimes expressed as a "whole-window" value including the effect of the frame. What is important is the ability to see through the glass,

not the frame, so be sure you get the VT of the glass, not of the entire unit.

The VT in residential windows extends from a shady 15 percent for some tinted glass up to 90 percent for clear glass. To most people, glass with VT values above 60 percent looks clear. Any value below 50 percent begins to look dark and/or reflective. Dariush Arasteh, staff scientist at Lawrence Berkeley Laboratory, warns, "People have very different perceptions of what is clear and what has a tint of color, especially when they look through glass at an angle." Look at a sample of glass outdoors and judge for yourself before you decide to order the window.

It's Warm in the Sun

Manufacturers have long used shading coefficient (SC) to describe how much solar heat their windows transmit. A totally opaque unit scores 0, and a single pane of clear glass scores 1 on this comparative scale. A clear double-pane window scores 0.84 because it allows 84 percent as much heat to pass as a single pane of glass.

Solar-heat-gain coefficient (SHGC) is the new, more accurate tool that is replacing SC to describe solar-heat gain. SHGC is the fraction of available solar heat that successfully passes through a window. It, too, uses a scale of 0, for none, to 1 for 100 percent of available light. The key difference is that SHGC is based on a percentage of available solar heat rather than on a percentage of what comes through a single pane of glass. It considers various sun angles and the shading effect of the window frame.

Glass coatings are formulated to select specific wavelengths of energy. It is possible to have a glass coating that blocks long-wave heat energy (low SHGC) while allowing generous amounts of visible light (high VT) to enter a home. This formulation is ideal in warm climates. A low SHGC can reduce air-conditioning bills more than if you increased the insulative value of your window with an additional pane of glass. I recommend a SHGC under 0.40 for hot climates. In cold climates, you want both high VT and high SHGC. I recommend an SHGC of 0.55 and above in the North. In swing climates such as Washington, D.C., choosing a SHGC between 0.40 and 0.55 is reasonable because there is a trade-off between cooling and heating loads. For people in swing climates, Arasteh suggests, "Think about your specific comfort needs when specifying SHGC. If you like wearing sweaters and hate being overheated in the summer, then a low SHGC may be the choice for you." Choose the blend of glass coatings that works best in your climate and exposure.

Preventing UV Damage

Windows that block UV-radiation reduce fabric fading. Expect to find windows off the shelf that block more than 75 percent of the UV energy. Contrary to conventional wisdom, some visible light fades fabric, too. Some manufacturers use the Krochmann Damage Function to rate a window's ability to limit fabric-fading potential. It expresses the percentage of both UV and of that portion of the visible spectrum that passes through the window and causes fading. Lower numbers are better.

Window manufacturers sometimes boast R-8 (U-0.125) values. Be careful. This may be the value only at the center of the glass, which is always artificially higher than the whole-unit value. Look for whole-unit values of U-0.33 or better. Some manufacturers stretch low-e-coated plastic film within the gas-filled airspace of double-glazed units to provide an effective third or fourth "pane." The weight of these windows is comparable to double glazing, and the true overall window performance is boosted to levels of U-0.17 or better for some. These units are pricey, but they can be more energy efficient

than walls in cold climates. The R-value is lower than a typical wall, but if triple-glazed units are designed with a high SHGC and are placed in a sunny wall, they can be net energy gainers.

Keeping Warm around the Edges

If you've lived in a cold climate, you've seen condensation and even frost on windows. When warm indoor air cools below its dew point, liquid water condenses on the glass. Condensation typically develops around the edges of window glass. No surprise. The edge is where most multiple-pane glazing is held apart by highly conductive aluminum spacers.

The coldest part of a multiple-glazed window is around its edges (see the chart on p. 142). It's worse with true divided-lite windows; because each lite has edge spacers, the ratio of cold edge to warm center is much higher than with regular insulated windows. Moist conditions support mold growth and hasten decay and paint failure. Condensation is the number 1 reason for window-related callbacks. Warm edges reduce the chance of condensation forming.

The material the spacer is made from affects the rate that heat travels through a window's edge. Many window makers now offer warm edge spacers as standard fare. Aluminum spacers are not acceptable. The best windows use less-conductive materials such as thin stainless steel, plastic, foam, and rubber. Warm edge spacers can improve the U-value of a window by 10 percent and boost the edge temperature by around 5°F, thereby reducing condensation.

TIP

Window manufacturers sometimes boast R-8 (U-0.125) values. Be careful. This may be the value only at the center of the glass. Look for the whole-unit values U-0.33 or better.

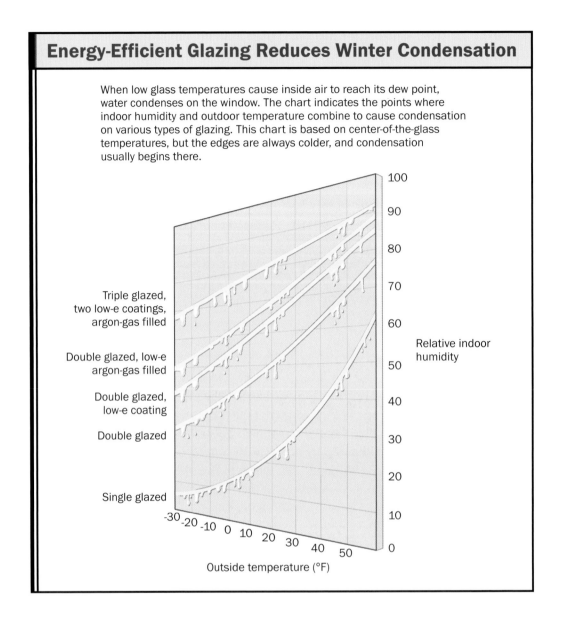

Energy-Efficient Glazing Reduces Winter Condensation

When low glass temperatures cause inside air to reach its dew point, water condenses on the window. The chart indicates the points where indoor humidity and outdoor temperature combine to cause condensation on various types of glazing. This chart is based on center-of-the-glass temperatures, but the edges are always colder, and condensation usually begins there.

Triple glazed, two low-e coatings, argon-gas filled

Double glazed, low-e argon-gas filled

Double glazed, low-e coating

Double glazed

Single glazed

Relative indoor humidity

Outside temperature (°F)

Good Frames Insulate

The most widely available window frames are wood (including vinyl-clad and aluminum-clad wood frames), with 46 percent of the market. Hollow vinyl frames hold 36 percent of the market, and aluminum runs a distant third, with a 17 percent market share. A trickle of alternative materials such as wood-resin composites, fiberglass, PVC foam, and insulated vinyl makes up another 1 percent of windows sold. A window's frame represents about 25 percent of its area. So it's important that the frame material be thermally nonconductive. For the most part, wood and vinyl are the best performers, and

they work equally well (see the chart on the facing page). Aluminum frames are typically poor energy performers.

Connections where the frame joins together must be tightly sealed to keep out water and air. Weatherstripping needs to seal tightly after hundreds of window closings, rain wettings, sun dryings, and winter freezings. Inexpensive, flimsy plastic, metal, or brushlike materials don't last. Compressible gaskets like those used to seal car doors are best. Closures must clinch windows tightly shut. Look carefully at these components, and ask your architect or builder about a particular brand's track record. Pick longtime winners. Let others experiment with a new brand.

Frame Materials also Affect Energy Performance

There is a great difference in the insulative value of common frame materials. Here are some typical U-values for common frame materials.

FRAME MATERIAL	U-VALUE
Aluminum (no thermal break)	1.9–2.2
Aluminum (with thermal break)	1.0
Aluminum-clad wood/reinforced vinyl	0.4–0.6
Wood and vinyl	0.3–0.5
Insulated vinyl/insulated fiberglass	0.2–0.3

Wood is typically the most expensive frame material. Maintenance is one of the biggest drawbacks to using solid-wood windows. Wood rots, shrinks, and swells. Paint fails. Solid wood requires frequent, fussy maintenance. On the other hand, well-maintained wood looks good, is stable, and can be recolored easily. Clad versions are the easiest to maintain. On the down side, if you get sick of the cladding color, too bad. When you choose either a solid or clad version, be sure that the manufacturer has treated its wood frames with water-repellent preservative to improve durability, paint retention, and dimensional stability.

Vinyl Windows Are Built to Move

Vinyl windows have been around for 35 years. Vinyl is energy efficient, durable, rotproof, insectproof, and weather resistant. It's made with chemicals that inhibit UV-degradation. Vinyl is colored throughout and requires no painting. The knock on vinyl is that it fades, can't be painted, becomes brittle with age, and is thermally unstable (especially dark colors). Temperature changes cause it to contract and expand more than wood, aluminum, and even the glass it holds. Vinyl frames have the potential for causing increased air leakage over time because of this movement. But Richard Walker, technical director of the American Architectural Manufacturers Association℠ (AAMA, 1827 Walden Office Square, Suite 104, Schaumberg, IL 60173; 847-303-5664), is quick to say, "Vinyl windows are built with this movement in mind, and failures have not been recorded to cause concern." If you choose vinyl frames, specify light colors and heat-welded corners. Heat-welded corners hold up best over time.

The pigments that are used in paint are almost identical to those used in vinyl, but vinyl's color goes all the way through. Walker says, "A little rubdown with Soft Scrub or one of the products on our [AAMA] list of recommended cleaners will bring vinyl back to its original brilliance." I tried the Soft Scrub test and was impressed with how much brighter aged vinyl became. Not the original color, to be sure, but the scrubbing resulted in a marked improvement.

Fiberglass-frame windows are showing up in a few product lines. Fiberglass is extremely strong, and because it is made of glass fibers, the frames and the glass expand at the same rate. Fiberglass must be painted and is more expensive than vinyl. Owens

Verifying Energy Performance

Until recently, purchasing a window was a little bit like buying a mattress. With mattresses you get cushion firm, "chiro protector," and Posturepedic plus. Huh? With windows you're promised energy performance with U- and R-values. But what does the advertised R-value mean? And does it mean the same for all windows? Hardly. Some manufacturers determine R-value by measuring conductance at a single point in the center of the glass and do not count heat transferred through the frame or through metal spacers at the edges of the window. They do not account for the air that leaks around the sash. Nor do they measure radiant-heat loss from the entire window unit. Others honestly report whole-window values.

In 1989, the National Fenestration Rating Council (NFRC) was formed to level the playing field in the window industry. NFRC's mission is to develop a national energy-performance rating system for windows and doors. All NFRC-rated windows are tested using a reliable, standard procedure that measures energy transfer through the entire window unit. U-values, solar heat gain coefficients, visible-light transmittance values, and air-leakage rates are now (or will be soon) listed on certified windows. When consumers see an NFRC label on the windows they are considering, they can be sure that they have a reliable tool they can use to compare windows.

As of June 1997, NFRC had over 150 participants with more than 30,000 windows, doors, and sky-lights in the program. "This includes all of the major manufacturers like Jeld-Wen, Andersen, Marvin, Pella, Certainteed, Owens Corning, Peachtree, etc.," says Susan Douglas, the NFRC's administrative director.

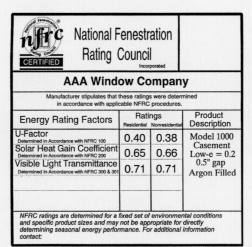

All NFRC-rated windows have this label. Manufacturers must list U-value, but other values are optional. Tests used to determine the values are consistent, so this label is useful for comparing different manufacturers' windows.

RULES OF THUMB FOR WINDOW SELECTION
To get the best value from your windows, select units that match your climate. This chart suggests minimum values for the listed climates.

	Madison, WI (7,643 heating degree days)	St. Louis, MO (4,948 heating degree days)	 Phoenix, AZ (1,444 heating degree days)
U-VALUE	< 0.33	0.33	0.33
VISUAL TRANSMISSIONS	50%	> 50%	> 60%
SOLAR HEAT GAIN COEFFICIENT	0.40–0.55	> 0.55	< 0.40
UV PROTECTION	> 75%	75%	75%
EDGE SPACERS	Warm edge spacers	Warm edge spacers	< 0.33
FRAME	Nonconductive frames	Nonconductive frames	Nonconductive frames
AIR LEAKAGE	< 0.30 cfm/ft^2.	< 0.30 cfm/ft^2.	< 0.30 cfm/ft^2.

1. U-values influence heat loss more in cold climates because the differrences between indoor and outdoor temperatures are much greater than in hot climates.
2. Consider trade-offs involving comfort and performance in swing climates.

How the NFRC System Works

Window manufacturers that want to be certified hire a NFRC-accredited lab. The lab simulates the thermal performance of the windows with computers. Entire unit performance—including frame, spacer, and glass—is measured. Windows with the highest and lowest simulated U-values in each product line (such as casements) are physically tested to verify the computer simulation. An independent NFRC-licensed inspection agency reviews the computer simulations and randomly pulls window units from the factory floor as test samples. Physical test values must fall within 10 percent of the computer predictions for a product line to be validated.

Presently, manufacturers that participate in the NFRC program must include certified U-values on the label. They also elect whether to include solar heat gain, coefficient visible-light transmittance, and emissivity on the label. NFRC has created a technical procedure to measure air leakage and expected to have the details ironed out by January 1998. Douglas promises, "You can expect air-leakage values soon." Solar heat gain is based solely on computer simulation, while visible transmittance, air leakage and emittance are physically measured values. The NFRC does not evaluate durability now, but the group does have a long-term performance subcommittee in place and expects to consider durability in the future.

Certified products have temporary and permanent markings. The big, temporary label is placed in a highly visible spot on the window. A small permanent NFRC serial code is etched on an inconspicuous part of the window, such as a spacer or metal strip. Permanent labels are useful. Potential buyers of older homes often ask, "What kind of windows are these?" A phone call to the NFRC will provide the brand and rating for the unit. Labels provide builders, designers, code officials, and consumers with information needed to verify code compliance and a reliable level of performance.

Beyond Labels

RESFEN, a computer program developed by Lawrence Berkeley Laboratory, enables you to minimize energy use, maximize comfort, control glare, and maximize natural lighting in your home design. Builders, architects, or consumers who want to fine-tune a design and choose specific windows for specific exposures on a house in a particular climate can order *RESFEN* from the NFRC for about $15. *The NFRC Certified Product Directory* and *RESFEN* are available from NFRC, 1300 Spring St., Suite 500, Silver Spring, MD 20910; 301-589-6372.

Corning®, Andersen, and Marvin are three major manufacturers that produce fiberglass windows. Owens Corning is the only manufacturer that makes fiberglass windows with insulated frames. But before you get too excited, the whole-window U-value for a low-e argon-filled casement window carries the same 0.32 rating for both an uninsulated vinyl and an insulated fiberglass unit.

Aluminum-frame windows are durable, requiring little maintenance. However, they are energy siphons and shouldn't be used where energy efficiency is a consideration.

The range of window options available today is staggering. But a working knowledge of the terms and these few guidelines should make choosing windows a little less intimidating (see the chart on the facing page).

You might also want to get ahold of this book: *Residential Windows: A Guide to New Technologies and Energy Performance* by John Carmody and co-authors (W. W. Norton, 1996).

*Note prices are from 1998.

Paul Fisette is director of the Building Materials Technology and Management Program at the University of Massachusetts in Amherst.

Reglazing Windows and Doors

■ WILLIAM T. COX JR.

I recently remodeled an old home 20 miles outside of Memphis. I needed to head back over to the place to finish off a small punch list. Among the items on the list were a couple of panes of glass that needed replacing. The broken panes were in the wooden double-hung windows in the front of the house, plus a pane broken out of a wooden side door. The job wasn't big enough to call in a glass company, so in addition to my regular tools, I loaded my van with some stock sizes of single-strength glass, a box of points, and a can of glazing compound.

Gloves May Help in Removing Broken Glass

Reglazing is simple as long as the proper tools and techniques are used. The first step is removing the broken pieces of glass as carefully as possible, remembering that the edge of broken glass is sharper than any cutting tool (see the left photo on the facing page). The Occupational Safety and Health Administration (OSHA) recommends that gloves be worn at all times when handling glass, but having learned how to handle glass from my uncle, I feel safer being able to feel the glass with bare hands. A lot of the glaziers I've talked to swear by the gummy gloves that are made for handling glass. The debate over gloves will probably go on forever, but there are no good reasons for not wearing eye protection. Safety glasses or goggles should be worn at all times, especially when removing the glass shards of a broken pane.

After all of the loose pieces of glass are taken out, I remove the old putty. If the windows haven't been reglazed in a while, the putty usually separates from the wood fairly easily. If the old putty is stuck to the wood, a sharp utility knife and small scraper will remove it. I also carry an old bottle/can opener to get rid of hardest stuff (see the right photo on the facing page). The sharpened point of the opener will get into even the smallest cracks.

While removing the glass and old putty, I often come across tiny, flat, diamond-shaped pieces of metal. These things are glazing

Sharp as a razor. Shards of broken glass are incredibly sharp, and special care needs to be taken when removing these pieces from the frame.

An old tool with a new job. A bottle/can opener with a sharpened point works great to scrape out the most stubborn old putty that hangs on to the wooden frame.

points, shot into the frame at the factory by a tool similar to a stapling gun. Glazing points hold the glass in the openings of the frames. The putty or glazing compound is meant only to seal the glass from air and moisture infiltration. Without the points, the glass would simply fall out over time. Factory points can be saved and put back in, but replacement points are cheap and go in easily.

When the opening is cleaned to the bare wood, I measure it side to side and top to bottom and deduct ⅛ in. in each direction for the glass size. The top panes in the bottom sash of a double-hung window are the exception to this rule. The bottom sash has a slit running along the top stile for the panes to slide into. The top-to-bottom measurement for these panes needs to be ⅛ in. larger than the opening. Just ⅛ in. of play in each direction should work for all openings that are straight and true. For windows

that are badly out of square, I need to figure out whether it's best to replace the broken pane, replace the sash, or buy a whole new window.

If more than a couple of panes of glass need replacing, it may be more convenient to take the sash out and repair them on sawhorses. Be aware that removing the sash will create additional work because the sash stops, cords, or universal slides will need to be removed and the inside trim will probably have to be repainted later.

A good cut starts with the right grip. Holding the glass cutter properly is the first key to successful cutting. Apply even pressure and draw the cutter back with a single smooth, continuous motion.

Cutting glass is a snap. After scoring the glass, grip it on both sides of the score mark and apply firm pressure. The pane should break smoothly along the score.

A Little Light Oil Makes Glass Cutting a Lot Easier

I'm a little leery of hardware stores that sell glass on the side. These places have a contraption that aligns and cuts the glass in one smooth motion. However, I've gotten glass cut on these machines that was so out of square that it wouldn't fit into the opening. A glass shop has all of the equipment needed for precise glass cutting: a flat, cushioned table; a selection of T-squares; oil; and, of course, the best glass-cutting tools. But because there were only a few pieces of glass to install for this project, I decided to cut my own glass on a table made from a piece of plywood on top of my sawhorses. I used an 18-in. ruler for a straightedge.

Glass cutting always goes a lot easier with a very sharp cutting wheel on the glass cutter and a little machine oil. Until the late 1960s, glass cutters were expensive and made with replaceable cutting wheels. Now, with the whole tool costing only a couple of dollars, I keep a new glass cutter handy for each glazing job I do. The machine oil lubricates the cutting wheel, and a little oil laid on the glass just before cutting will prevent a "hot" cut (chunks and shards of glass splintering from the scoring).

Cutting the glass to the right size the first time will save a lot of headaches. Thin strips of glass are difficult to take off with a glass cutter. If I need to fine-tune a glass cut, my belt sander with a 120-grit belt will take off small amounts.

The proper grip on the glass cutter will also help with getting a good cut. Most glass cutters should be held with the handle between the middle and the index fingers and the tip of the index finger and thumb gripping the handle just above the cutting wheel (see the top photo at left). If this position feels too odd, hold the cutter like a pencil; either method will give excellent control of the tool.

Start with the cutter wheel at the edge of the glass and press down until the wheel digs in slightly. Then, with a smooth and continuous motion, score the glass, listening for a long, even, rasping sound as you cut. It's the same principle as hitting the perfect golf shot: It has to be right the first time.

Marks on glass are tough to see and rub off easily, so when I'm ready to cut a piece of glass, I measure with a steel tape and move my straightedge to get the measurement without making marks on the glass. I adjust my measurement to allow for the thickness of the glass cutter, dip the cutter in oil and score the glass once and only once. Scoring the glass more than once may cause it to shatter, or the cut will be ragged at best. Then I pick up the sheet of glass quickly, gripping each side of the score mark with my thumbs on top and index fingers underneath. I apply firm pressure on both sides of the score mark and snap the glass (see the bottom photo on the facing page). It's necessary to snap glass quickly once it is scored because glass is a super-cooled liquid. Scoring the glass disturbs its molecules, and the glass will snap more readily while the molecules of glass are still moving around.

Give the Bare Frame a Coat of Linseed Oil before Glazing

I always dry-fit the pane and then lay it aside. With a rag I rub a good coat of linseed oil on all bare wood surfaces (see the top photo at right). Linseed oil is a vegetable oil and one of the main ingredients of glazing compound. Linseed oil refreshes the wood and stops the oil from being wicked out of the newly applied putty. Some folks recommend priming the bare wood with latex paint. I think this does more harm than good because it provides a path between the putty and the wood for air and moisture to get in.

Prep the bare wood with linseed oil. Linseed oil refreshes the wood and keeps the wood from drawing the oil out of the putty.

Warming up the putty. Knead a ball of putty about the size of an egg to warm it and make it soft and workable.

Glazing points are pushed in with a putty knife. With the glass set in the frame, glazing points are inserted to keep the pane in place. Tiny vertical tabs on the points let you use a putty knife to push the points into the wood.

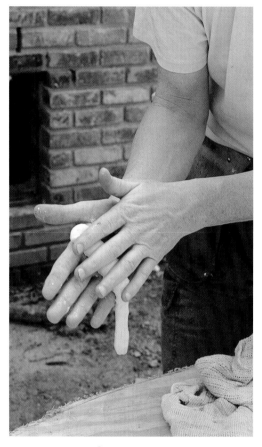

A putty rope is easier to work into the frame. Roll the putty between your hands, and use your fingers to press it into the sash.

A smooth putty knife removes the excess. Drawing a smooth, clean putty knife along each side of the window at the proper angle presses the compound into place, smooths it out, and takes off any excess. The proper angle is determined by the height and depth of the rabbet.

I dig out a wad of putty about the size of an egg and knead it until it becomes warm and pliable (see the bottom photo on p. 149). If the original piece of glass was back-bedded, I apply a thin layer of putty on the inside lip of the sash (or muntins) and then press the glass into the putty. Next I install two glazing points along each side of the glass pane (see the top right photo on the facing page). I roll the putty between both hands until it resembles a short piece of thick rope (see the left photo on the facing page), and work this putty rope into the angle between the glass and the mullion. I apply a liberal amount of putty along all four sides with my fingers before I get out my putty knife.

The putty knife should be as clean and as smooth as possible, which is why a lot of them are made with chrome-plated blades. The blade of the knife should also be flexible. With the putty knife, I press the glazing compound into place as I smooth it out and remove the excess putty (see the bottom right photo on the facing page). If the putty knife isn't smooth and clean, it will pull the putty away from the wood. Proper technique is the secret.

I hold the putty knife at a slight angle to the frame, and with a steady backward stroke, I "wipe" the putty into place. The putty knife cuts away any excess; and at the same time, the blade pushes the glazing compound in at the proper angle, which is determined by the height and depth of the rabbet. The best way to smooth any remaining bumps or to close small cracks is to rub the putty lightly with your finger, which builds up a little heat and softens the putty slightly. Rubbing the putty with your finger also brings a little oil to the surface, which I believe aids in the curing of the glazing compound. After I'd finished glazing all of the new panes in the double-hung windows on the front of the house, I moved on to the side door.

Door Lites Must Be Replaced with Tempered Glass or Acrylic

The three-lite, three-panel door had been installed in the 1950s when the house was built, and vandals had recently broken one of the panes. Back in the 1950s, door glass did not have to be tempered. However, in 1977 a federal law was passed, mandating that all glass in and up to 1 ft. away from a door be tempered glass or acrylic sheet. It's up to the states, of course, to enforce the law, and here in Tennessee, the law states that anyone buying plain glass must sign a paper stating that the glass will not be used in a door. Before you replace any glass in a door, check your local building codes and the laws concerning door glass, but never use plain glass in a door.

As in most wooden doors, the panes of glass were held in place by wooden stops. With my utility knife I cut the paint away from the seams, or the wooden stops would never have come out in one piece. Tempered glass is impossible to cut, so I had to order the sizes I needed from a local glass company that specializes in tempered glass. After putting a small bead of silicon caulk on the back lip of the rabbet to keep the glass from rattling, I installed the glass and replaced the wooden stops, using 1-in. brads to hold them in place.

William T. Cox Jr. is a remodel/repair contractor in Memphis, Tennessee, and a frequent contributor to Fine Homebuilding.

CREDITS

INDEX

Taunton's FOR PROS BY PROS Series
A Collection of the best articles from *Fine Homebuilding* magazine

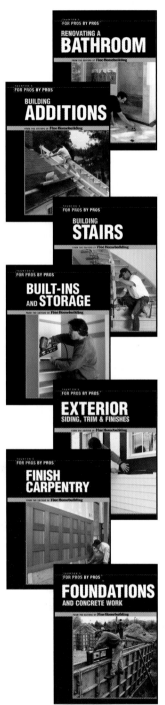

**Other books
in the series:**

**Taunton's For Pros By Pros:
RENOVATING A BATHROOM**

ISBN 1-56158-584-X
Product # 070702
$17.95 U.S.
$25.95 Canada

**Taunton's For Pros By Pros:
BUILDING ADDITIONS**

ISBN 1-56158-699-4
Product # 070779
$17.95 U.S.
$25.95 Canada

**Taunton's For Pros By Pros:
BUILDING STAIRS**

ISBN 1-56158-653-6
Product # 070742
$17.95 U.S.
$25.95 Canada

**Taunton's For Pros By Pros:
BUILT-INS AND STORAGE**

ISBN 1-56158-700-1
Product # 070780
$17.95 U.S.
$25.95 Canada

**Taunton's For Pros By Pros:
EXTERIOR SIDING,
TRIM & FINISHES**

ISBN 1-56158-652-8
Product # 070741
$17.95 U.S.
$25.95 Canada

**Taunton's For Pros By Pros:
FINISH CARPENTRY**

ISBN 1-56158-536-X
Product # 070633
$17.95 U.S.
$25.95 Canada

**Taunton's For Pros By Pros:
FOUNDATIONS AND
CONCRETE WORK**

ISBN 1-56158-537-8
Product # 070635
$17.95 U.S.
$25.95 Canada

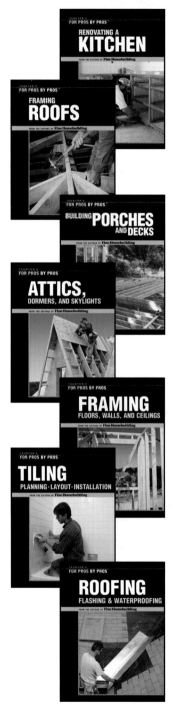

**Taunton's For Pros By Pros:
RENOVATING A KITCHEN**

ISBN 1-56158-540-8
Product # 070637
$17.95 U.S.
$25.95 Canada

**Taunton's For Pros By Pros:
FRAMING ROOFS**

ISBN 1-56158-538-6
Product # 070634
$17.95 U.S.
$25.95 Canada

**Taunton's For Pros By Pros:
BUILDING PORCHES
AND DECKS**

ISBN 1-56158-539-4
Product # 070636
$17.95 U.S.
$25.95 Canada

**Taunton's For Pros By Pros:
ATTICS, DORMERS,
AND SKYLIGHTS**

ISBN 1-56158-779-6
Product # 070834
$17.95 U.S.
$25.95 Canada

**Taunton's For Pros By Pros:
FRAMING FLOORS, WALLS,
AND CEILINGS**

ISBN 1-56158-758-3
Product # 070821
$17.95 U.S.
$25.95 Canada

**Taunton's For Pros By Pros:
TILING: PLANNING, LAYOUT,
INSTALLATION**

ISBN 1-56158-788-5
Product # 070843
$17.95 U.S.
$25.95 Canada

**Taunton's For Pros By Pros:
ROOFING, FLASHING &
WATERPROOFING**

ISBN 1-56158-778-8
Product # 070833
$17.95 U.S.
$25.95 Canada

For more information contact our website at: www.taunton.com